52
79 (typ)?
105
111
134?
141?
145

A ROLAND ALLEN READER

THE COMPULSION OF THE SPIRIT

Edited by
David Paton & Charles H. Long

William B. Eerdmans Publishing Company, *Grand Rapids, Michigan*
Forward Movement Publications, *Cincinnati, Ohio*

We gratefully acknowledge permission to reproduce excerpts from the following sources:

from *The Ministry of the Spirit*, ed. David M. Paton, copyright © 1960 by World Dominion Press

from *Missionary Methods: St. Paul's or Ours?*, by Roland Allen, copyright © 1962 by World Dominion Press

from *Reform of the Ministry*, ed. David M. Paton, copyright © 1968 by Lutterworth Press

from *The Spontaneous Expansion of the Church*, by Roland Allen, copyright © 1962 by World Dominion Press

Library of Congress Cataloging in Publication Data

Allen, Roland, 1869-1947.
The compulsion of the spirit.

Bibliography: p. 149
1. Missions —Addresses, essays, lectures. 2. Holy
Spirit —Addresses, essays, lectures. 3. Clergy —
Addresses, essays, lectures. I. Paton, David MacDonald.
II. Long, Charles H. III. Title.
BV2070.A4325 1983   266'.33   83-14006
ISBN 0-8028-1261-9

Contents

Preface

Roland Allen was born in 1868, the son of a priest of the Church of England who died when Allen was quite young. He went to Bristol Grammar School and St John's College, Oxford (with a scholarship), where he read Classics and Modern History and won the Lothian Prize. After Leeds Clergy Training School (whose Principal described him as 'a refined intellectual man, small not vigorous, in no way burly or muscular. . . . Learning and civilisation are more to him than most men') Allen was ordained and did a curacy. In 1895 he went to North China as a missionary of the moderately 'High Church' Society for the Propagation of the Gospel. After a period of language study, he was engaged first in the training of catechists and then as a district missionary. He was invalided home in 1903 and became Vicar of Chalfont St Peter in Buckinghamshire. He resigned from this post in 1907 and never afterwards held any official Anglican office.

Allen had already begun to question radically the methods in use at that peak of the missionary expansion of North Atlantic Christianity. In 1912 he published the probing *Missionary Methods: St Paul's or Ours?* In 1914 he met Sidney James Wells Clark, a successful businessman who was passionately committed to the Christian world mission. Clark founded the Survey Application Trust, whose twin purposes were to survey the progress made by Christian missions and to spread the ideas of Roland Allen through a variety of publications and the periodical *World Dominion*.

Allen was an Anglican High Churchman, to whom the ministry and the sacraments were of great importance; his associates in the S.A.T. were mostly Evangelical Protestants who did not easily understand his enthusiasm for voluntary clergy. Allen for his part did not see much point in surveying unevangelized fields if people were going to make in them the same mistakes they had made elsewhere, but his own enthusiasm for non-professional clergy was not taken up in the churches of the Anglican Communion. In 1932 he retired to Kenya, where his son was working, and settled there. He learned Swahili well enough to do some translations from that tongue into English. He died in 1947.

Roland Allen himself predicted that an interest in the ideas that preoccupied him would begin about 1960, and this did indeed prove to be the case. Moreover, action began to follow. This aroused awareness of Allen's ideas. In various ways, massive events like the communist revolution in China and the Mau Mau rebellion in Kenya raised questions about the foreignness and even sterility of much mission-controlled Christianity in Africa and Asia; and those who had to answer the questions found themselves turning to Allen's ideas — in the Church Growth movement, certainly, but not only there. On the ministry side, a shortage of full-time clergy and of money to pay them opened the way for the implementation of Allen's views; and in many Anglican dioceses there are now not only many 'non-stipendiary priests' but also the beginnings of a 'Locally Ordained Ministry' which is put up by the congregation and recognized by the Bishop and fostered by the Diocese.

This book contains the crucial parts of Allen's writing *for the times in which we live and share in the Christian mission.* Much water has passed under many bridges since 1943, when Allen wrote the latest of the writings we have included; still more since 1907, the date of the earliest piece, and 1895 when we sailed for China. The future will be something else again. Here we have collected those excerpts from Allen's writings that seemed most relevant for the concerns of our time in the minds of the American publishers of Allen's works and two Anglican priests, one American and one British, who like Roland Allen himself worked in China as missionaries in time of turmoil. If it is felt that a corrective is needed, it can be found by pursuing the books mentioned in the bibliography.

DAVID M. PATON
CHARLES LONG

I

MISSIONARY METHODS
AND
CHURCH GROWTH

This section includes the "Introduction" and chapter 13 ("Application") and chapter 14 ("Epilogue") from *Missionary Methods: St. Paul's or Ours?*, first published in 1912. From *The Spontaneous Expansion of the Church* (1927) there is the whole of the final chapter 9 ("The Way of Spontaneous Expansion") preceded by an editorial note summarizing Allen's line of thought in the earlier chapters of that book.

1

Introduction

In little more than ten years St Paul established the Church in
four provinces of the Empire, Galatia, Macedonia, Achaia and
Asia. Before AD 47 there were no churches in these provinces; in
AD 57 St Paul could speak as if his work there was done, and could
plan extensive tours into the far west without anxiety lest the churches
which he had founded might perish in his absence for want of his
guidance and support.

The work of the Apostle during these ten years can therefore be
treated as a unity. Whatever assistance he may have received from
the preaching of others, it is unquestioned that the establishment of
the churches in these provinces was really his work. In the pages of
the New Testament he, and he alone, stands forth as their founder.
And the work which he did was really a completed work. So far as
the foundation of the churches is concerned, it is perfectly clear that
the writer of the Acts intends to represent St Paul's work as complete.
The churches were really established. Whatever disasters fell upon
them in later years, whatever failure there was, whatever ruin, that
failure was not due to any insufficiency or lack of care and complete-
ness in the Apostle's teaching or organization. When he left them he
left them because his work was fully accomplished.

This is truly an astonishing fact. That churches should be founded
so rapidly, so securely, seems to us today, accustomed to the difficulties, the uncertainties, the failures, the disastrous relapses of our
own missionary work, almost incredible. Many missionaries in later
days have received a larger number of converts than St Paul; many
have preached over a wider area than he; but none have so established churches. We have long forgotten that such things could be.
We have long accustomed ourselves to accept it as an axiom of
missionary work that converts in a new country must be submitted
to a very long probation and training, extending over generations
before they can be expected to be able to stand alone. Today if a
man ventures to suggest that there may be something in the methods
by which St Paul attained such wonderful results worthy of our care-

3

ful attention, and perhaps of our imitation, he is in danger of being accused of revolutionary tendencies.

Yet this is manifestly not as it should be. It is impossible but that the account so carefully given by St Luke of the planting of the churches in the Four Provinces should have something more than a mere archaeological and historical interest. Like the rest of the Holy Scriptures it was 'written for our learning'. It was certainly meant to be something more than the romantic history of an exceptional man, doing exceptional things under exceptional circumstances—a story from which ordinary people of a later age can get no more instruction for practical missionary work than they receive from the history of the Cid, or from the exploits of King Arthur. It was really intended to throw light on the path of those who should come after.

But it is argued that as a matter of fact St Paul was an exceptional man living in exceptional times, preaching under exceptional circumstances; that he enjoyed advantages in his birth, his education, his call, his mission, his relationship to his hearers, such as have been enjoyed by no other; and that he enjoyed advantages in the peculiar constitution of society at the moment of his call such as to render his work quite exceptional. To this I must answer: (1) That St Paul's missionary method was not peculiarly St Paul's, he was not the only missionary who went about establishing churches in those early days. The method in its broad outlines was followed by his disciples, and they were not all men of exceptional genius. It is indeed universal, and outside the Christian Church has been followed by reformers, religious, political, social, in every age and under most diverse conditions. It is only because he was a supreme example of the spirit, and power with which it can be used, that we can properly call the method St Paul's. (2) That we possess today an advantage of inestimable importance in that we have the printing press and the whole of the New Testament where St Paul had only the Old Testament in Greek. (3) That however highly we may estimate St Paul's personal advantages or the assistance which the conditions of his age afforded, they cannot be so great as to rob his example of all value for us. In no other work do we set the great masters wholly on one side, and teach the students of today that whatever they may copy, they may not copy them, because they lived in a different age under exceptional circumstances and were endowed with exceptional genius. It is just because they were endowed with exceptional genius that we say their work is endowed with a universal character. Either we must drag down St Paul from his pedestal as the great missionary, or else we must acknowledge that there is in his work that quality of universality.

The cause which has created this prejudice against the study of the Pauline method is not far to seek. It is due to the fact that every unworthy, idle and slip-shod method of missionary work has been fathered upon the Apostle. Men have wandered over the world, 'preaching the Word', laying no solid foundations, establishing nothing permanent, leaving no really instructed society behind them, and have claimed St Paul's authority for their absurdities. They have gone through the world, spending their time in denouncing ancient religions, in the name of St Paul. They have wandered from place to place without any plan or method of any kind, guided in their movements by straws and shadows, persuaded they were imitating St Paul on his journey from Antioch to Troas. Almost every intolerable abuse that has ever been known in the mission field has claimed some sentence or act of St Paul as its original.

It is in consequence of this, because in the past we have seen missionary work made ridiculous or dangerous by the vagaries of illiterate or unbalanced imitators of the Apostle, that we have allowed ourselves to be carried to the opposite extreme, and to shut our eyes to the profound teaching and practical wisdom of the Pauline method.

Secondly, people have adopted fragments of St Paul's method and have tried to incorporate them into alien systems, and the failure which resulted has been used as an argument against the Apostle's method. For instance, people have baptized uninstructed converts and the converts have fallen away; but St Paul did not baptize uninstructed converts apart from a system of mutual responsibility which ensured their instruction. Again, they have gathered congregations and have left them to fend for themselves, with the result that the congregations have fallen back into heathenism. But St Paul did not gather congregations, he planted churches, and he did not leave a church until it was fully equipped with orders of ministry, sacraments and tradition. Or again, they have trusted native helpers with the management of mission funds, and these helpers have grievously misused them; but St Paul did not do this. He had no funds with which to entrust anyone. These people have committed funds in trust to individual native helpers and have been deceived; but St Paul left the church to manage its own finance. These people have made the helpers responsible to *them* for honest management; but St Paul never made any church render an account of its finances to him. Or again, Europeans have ordained ill-educated native helpers and have repented of it. But they have first broken the bonds which should have united those whom they ordained to those to whom they were to minister, and then have expected them to be ministers of a foreign system of church organization with which neither the ministers nor their congregations were familiar. St Paul did not do this. He ordained ministers of the Church for the Church, and he instituted no elaborate constitution. When these false and partial attempts at imitating the Apostle's method have failed, men have declared that the apostolic method was at fault and was quite unsuited to the condition and circumstances of present-day missions. The truth is that they have neither understood nor practised the Apostle's method at all.

There is yet another and a more weighty reason: St Paul's method is not in harmony with the modern Western spirit. We modern teachers from the West are by nature and by training persons of restless activity and boundless self-confidence. We are accustomed to assume an attitude of superiority towards all Eastern peoples, and to point to our material progress as the justification of our attitude. We are accustomed to do things ourselves for ourselves, to find our own way, to rely upon our own exertions, and we naturally tend to be impatient with others who are less restless and less self-assertive than we are. We are accustomed by long usage to an elaborate system of church organization, and a peculiar code of morality. We cannot imagine any Christianity worthy of the name existing without the elaborate machinery which we have invented. We naturally expect our converts to adopt from us not only essentials but accidentals. We desire to impart not only the Gospel, but the Law and the Customs. With that spirit, St Paul's methods do not agree, because they were the natural outcome of quite another spirit, the spirit which preferred persuasion to authority. St Paul distrusted elaborate systems of religious ceremonial, and grasped fundamental principles with an unhesitating faith in the power of the Holy Ghost to apply them to his hearers and to work out their appropriate external expressions in them. It was inevitable that methods which were the natural outcome of the mind of St Paul should appear as dangerous to us as they appeared to the Jewish Christians of his own day. The mere fact that they can be made to bear a shallow resemblance to the methods of no method is sufficient to make the 'apostles of order' suspicious. In spite of the manifest fact that the Catholic Church was founded by them, they appear uncatholic to those who live in daily terror of schism. It seems almost as if we thought it uncatholic to establish the Church too fast.

But that day is passing. In face of the vast proportions of the work to be done, we are day by day seeking for some new light on the great problem how we may establish the Catholic Church in the world. In this search, the example of the Apostle of the Gentiles must be of the first importance to us. He succeeded in doing what we so far have only tried to do. The facts are unquestionable. In a very few years, he built the Church on so firm a basis that it could live and grow in faith and in practice, that it could work out its own problems, and overcome all dangers and hindrances both from within and without. I propose in this book to attempt to set forth the methods which he used to produce this amazing result.

I am not writing a book on St Paul's doctrine. I do not feel it necessary to argue over again the foundations of the faith. I am a churchman, and I write as a churchman. I naturally use terms which imply church doctrine. But the point to which I want to call attention is not the doctrine, which has been expounded and defended by many, but the Apostle's method. A true understanding of the method does not depend upon a true interpretation of the doctrine, but upon a true appreciation of the facts. About the facts there is very general agreement: about the doctrine there is very little agreement. E.g.— It is almost universally agreed that St Paul taught his converts the rite of baptism: it is very far from agreed what he meant by baptism. I use about baptism the terms of the Church of which I am a member. but my argument would be equally applicable if I used terms which implied a Zwinglian doctrine. Similarly I use about the orders of the ministry the terms natural to one who believes in apostolic succession. But the general force of my argument would not be affected if I used the terms natural to a Presbyterian or a Wesleyan. I suppose that I should scarcely need to alter more than a word or two, if I believed in 'the Churches' as firmly as I believe in 'the Church'. I hope, then, that, if I am happy enough to find readers who do not accept my ecclesiastical position, they will not allow themselves to be led away into the wilds of a controversy which I have tried as far as possible to exclude; and will rather seek to consider the method of the Apostle's work which I set forth than to find fault with the use of terms or expressions which imply a doctrine which they do not hold.

Neither am I attempting to describe the character of the Apostle or his special qualifications for the work, or his special preparation for it, still less am I attempting to write his life. I propose to deal simply with the foundation of the churches in the four provinces of Galatia, Macedonia, Achaia, Asia, in the ten years which covered the three missionary journeys. I wish to suggest an answer to the following questions:

I. Was there any antecedent advantage in the position or character of the cities in which St Paul founded his churches?

We must inquire:

(1) Whether he deliberately selected certain strategic points at which to establish his churches?

(2) Whether his success was due to the existence of some peculiar class of people to which he made a special appeal?

(3) Whether the social, moral or religious condition of the provinces was so unlike anything known in modern times, as to render futile any comparison between his work and ours.

II. Was there any peculiar virtue in the way in which the Apostle presented his gospel? Under this heading we must consider: (1) His use of miracles; (2) His finance; (3) The substance of his preaching.

III. Was there any peculiar virtue in the teaching which he gave to his converts or in his method of training his converts for baptism, or for ordination?

IV. Was there any peculiar virtue in his method of dealing with his organized churches? This will include the means by which (a) discipline was exercised and (b) unity maintained.

I shall try to point out as occasion offers where and how far we now follow or refuse the Apostle's method. It will, of course, be impossible and inadvisable to quote particular instances from the mission field. I can only deal in general terms with tendencies which will, I think, be quite familiar to any one who is acquainted with the missionary work of the present day.

V. Finally, I shall call attention to certain principles which seem to lie at the back of all the Apostle's actions and in which I believe we may find the key to his success, and endeavour to show some at least of the ways in which the apostolic method might be usefully employed today.

2

Application

The question may well be asked, How far is it possible to follow today the Apostle's methods which I have tried to set forth in the preceding chapters? It is plain that our Missions have hitherto proceeded on very different lines. Is it possible then to make any useful deductions? Is it possible to introduce into our Missions any of these methods without destroying to the very foundations all that we have hitherto established?

We have seen that the secret of the Apostle's success in founding churches lay in the observance of principles which we can reduce to rules of practice in some such form as this.

(1) All teaching to be permanent must be intelligible and so capable of being grasped and understood that those who have once received it can retain it, use it, and hand it on. The test of all teaching is practice. Nothing should be taught which cannot be so grasped and used.

(2) All organization in like manner must be of such a character that it can be understood and maintained. It must be an organization of which the people see the necessity: it must be an organization which they can and will support. It must not be so elaborate or so costly that small and infant communities cannot supply the funds necessary for its maintenance. The test of all organizations is naturalness and permanence. Nothing should be established as part of the ordinary church life of the people which they cannot understand and carry on.

(3) All financial arrangements made for the ordinary life and existence of the church should be such that the people themselves can and will control and manage their own business independently of any foreign subsidies. The management of all local funds should be entirely in the hands of the local church which should raise and use their own funds for their own purposes that they may be neither pauperized nor dependent on the dictation of any foreign society.

(4) A sense of mutual responsibility of all the Christians one for another should be carefully inculcated and practised. The whole community is responsible for the proper administration of baptism, ordination and discipline.

(5) Authority to exercise spiritual gifts should be given freely and at once. Nothing should be withheld which may strengthen the life of the church, still less should anything be withheld which is necessary for its spiritual sustenance. The liberty to enjoy such gifts is not a privilege which

may be withheld but a right which must be acknowledged. The test of preparedness to receive the authority is the capacity to receive the grace.

We have seen further that the power in which St Paul was able to act with such boldness was the spirit of faith. Faith, not in the natural capacities of his converts, but in the power of the Holy Ghost in them.

Now if we are to practise any methods approaching to the Pauline methods in power and directness, it is absolutely necessary that we should first have this faith, this Spirit. Without faith—faith in the Holy Ghost, faith in the Holy Ghost in our converts—we can do nothing. We cannot possibly act as the Apostle acted until we recover this faith. Without it we shall be unable to recognize the grace of the Holy Spirit in our converts, we shall never trust them, we shall never inspire in them confidence in the power of the Holy Spirit in themselves. If we have no faith in the power of the Holy Spirit in them, they will not learn to have faith in the power of the Holy Spirit in themselves. We cannot trust them, and they cannot be worthy of trust; and trust, the trust which begets trustworthiness, is the one essential for any success in the Pauline method.

But if we make that great venture of faith then the application of the Pauline method is still beset with difficulties because the past history of our converts is, as I have pointed out, very different from the history of his converts. Most missionaries today find themselves in charge of mission stations in the midst of established communities of Christians with often a long tradition of foreign government and foreign support behind them. Those communities will probably look to the missionary in everything. He is assisted by a number of native clergy, catechists and teachers whose work it is his duty to superintend. These again will look to him for guidance and encouragement, and probably for definite and particular orders in every conceivable circumstance that may arise, even if they do not depend upon his initiative and inspiration to save them from stagnation. In the central station he will almost certainly find a considerable organization and elaborate establishment which the native Christian community has not created and cannot at present support without financial aid from abroad. He will find that they have been more or less crammed with a complete system of theological and ecclesiastical doctrines which they have not been able to digest. He will find an elaborate system of finance which makes him in the last resort responsible for the raising and administration of all funds in his district. He will find that as regards baptism, the recommendation of candidates for office in the church, and the exercise of discipline, the whole burden of responsibility is laid upon his shoulders alone. He will find in a word that he is expected to act as an almost uncontrolled autocrat subject only to the admonitions of his bishop or the directions of a committee of white men.

He cannot possibly ignore that situation. He cannot act as if the Christian community over which he is called to preside had had another history. He cannot desert them and run away to some untouched field. He cannot begin all over again.

Nevertheless, if he has the Spirit of St Paul he can in a very real sense practise the method of St Paul in its nature, if not in its form. He cannot undo the past, but he can amend the present. He can keep ever before his mind the truth that he is there to prepare the way for the retirement of the foreign missionary. He can live his life amongst his people and deal with them *as though he would have no successor*. He should remember that he is the least permanent element in the church. He may fall sick and go home, or he may die, or he may be called elsewhere. He disappears, the church remains. The native Christians are the permanent element. The permanence of the church depends upon them. Therefore, it is of vital importance that if he is removed they should be able to carry on the work, as if he were present. He cannot rely, and he ought not to rely, upon having any successor. In many cases it must be literally true that he has none, at any rate, for some years. The supply of men from home is happily so inadequate that it is impossible to ensure a sufficient number of European recruits to man all the existing stations. It is obvious that there will not be, and ought not to be, enough to man similar stations all over any great country. In some cases it is probable that he will have no successor: in every case it is desirable that no successor should be necessary to the existence of the church.[1] Consequently, it is of the first importance that he should keep this always before him and strive by all means to secure that the absence of a

[1] This is what gives its peculiar sadness to the recurring appeals of our bishops for men to superintend missions which have been founded for many years. They are appeals not for a cure, but for a palliative. They are simply attempts to put off the evil day. There is in them no recognition of the evil, no resolve to meet and to overcome it, but only a desire to escape from it. The appeal today is the prophecy of another appeal a few years hence.

foreign superintendent should not result in that deplorable lapse from Christianity which we have only too often observed, with shame and grief, to follow upon the withdrawal of foreign support in the past. It is his first duty to prepare the way for the safe retirement of the foreign missionary.

He can do this in two ways: (1) He can associate the people with himself in all that he does and so make them thoroughly understand the nature of the work, and (2) he can practise retirement.

(1) *He can associate the people with himself in all that he does.* He need not do anything without their co-operation. By that I mean not merely that he can associate with himself a few individuals who seem suited to his mind, but that he can educate the whole congregation. In the past we have associated with ourselves individuals of our own selection, we have begun our education from the top. What is needful is to begin from the bottom. Leaders must be thrown up by the community, not dragged up by the missionary. It is necessary to make the whole body realize its unity and common responsibility. It is essential that he should not allow, he certainly must not encourage, the whole body to abandon all its responsibility to others, as he certainly will do if he deals only with a few people whom he has selected. He may avoid this danger by referring all business to the whole congregation in the first instance. In this way he will not only force the whole congregation to understand its responsibility, he will also compel those who are naturally leaders to understand that just as he cannot act as an autocrat because he has been put over them by the bishop, so neither can they so act because they have attracted his attention by some display of intellectual or social superiority. It is essential that the whole body should grow together. Now in doing this we shall find that the missionary must, in fact, follow the example of St Paul very nearly, as we shall see if we take a few instances. Let us take four typical examples of the Pauline method: the management of funds, the administration of baptism, the selection of ministers for the congregation, the exercise of discipline.

(a) *Finance.* It is important that the missionary should educate the whole congregation in the principles of church finance because this is a question which touches every member directly in a very obvious way, and when the people learn to understand that the control of finance is in their own hands they will more easily and quickly learn their responsibility in other matters. Even where, as in some central stations, a considerable proportion of the annual income is derived from foreign sources we need not hesitate to take this course. The missionary can teach the congregation as a congregation the sources from which all money is derived. He can make them understand what money is wanted and why it is wanted. He can generally give them control of all local expenses. He need not take charge of any money collected by the congregation even at their instant and special desire. He can refuse to accept the administration of money for which he is wholly and solely responsible. The modern institution of church councils will greatly assist him in this, but in the actual administration of money in small communities he need not even use a council. He can easily teach the whole community; for finance is a subject in which the whole congregation is naturally interested. If the people appoint a council to administer local funds, the council may be responsible to them primarily, and the use and abuse of funds may still be really in their hands. Only here is it unfortunately necessary to remark that it is no use to pretend. To consult the people whilst the missionary intends to carry out his own plans to hand over money to them and to keep control over it at the same time, is fatal. The people at once see the deception and resent it. They must be allowed to learn by making their own mistakes.

Of all local finance the administration of charity is the simplest and most instructive. The relief of distress should be entirely in the hands of the congregation. The creation of a charity committee is not so good an educational method in a small community as is the alleviation of individual cases as they arise by the whole congregation. Cases of poverty may be referred at once to the whole congregation. Everybody knows everybody else. The congregation knows exactly what is needed. They can reject the appeal or subscribe to meet it on the spot. The missionary, if he will, may subscribe with the others. Nothing is more calculated to draw the congregation together and to help the people to realize their mutual dependence, than the supply of special needs by special acts of charity one towards another. A poor fund, if it is administered by a missionary, only tends to misunderstanding and discontent.

Even in such matters as the foundation of schools, the congregation ought to manage its own business. The first thing is to persuade the people of the need for a school. Until they desire it and are ready to support it, nothing is done. When they want it, they will certainly seek the missionary's help. He can give help, why should he insist upon control? He and they, they and he, should think out the plans, seek for sources of supply, and engage the teacher. It is essential that the people should recognize that the school is their own school, not simply his. If he does the work for them, even though he may induce them to subscribe, the work will be his work not theirs, and they will feel no responsibility for its success or failure.[1]

Similarly, if a school is to be enlarged the missionary has another opportunity of teaching his people the same lesson. The school is really their school, not his, even if it has been founded in the first instance with foreign money. It is their children who are to be educated in it. They are really more nearly affected by the alteration than we are. Then they should be consulted, and their advice should be taken. It is a grievous loss to the whole Church if the work is done simply by foreigners, when the whole community might be made to realize, as perhaps they never realized before, its importance to them and their responsibility for it.

In finance, as in other matters, the principle of throwing upon the shoulders of the native Christians all the responsibility that they can carry, and more than they can carry, is a sound one. If they have more than they can manage, they will gladly seek advice and help; if they have less, they will, sooner or later, begin to fight for more or to feel aggrieved that they are not given their proper place.

(b) *Baptism*. The admission of new converts is a matter which very intimately affects the whole Church. It cannot but seriously affect

---

[1] There is one aspect of this question which I can only refer to with grief and shame, but I dare not omit it. I am afraid that there are congregations who have been so ill-educated by us in the past that they would be ready to sell themselves to the highest bidder. If they were free, and thought that they could get larger grants from another mission, they would go over. If they wanted help to build or enlarge schools more than their own missionary could supply, they would threaten to accept help from some other society. And I fear that there are Christian missions which would offer them such help for the sake of augmenting their numbers. In such cases we should have to consider carefully whether it was worth while to keep them at the price. They ought to have the case set clearly before them, and obviously it is essential that they should know and feel that the missionary is solely devoted to securing their true welfare. But if they resolve to sell themselves to another Society for a school, they should be prevented from so doing by no other than moral persuasion, and I cannot believe that many congregations would accept the bait held out to them, if they saw that their liberty and self-respect were involved. But, in the last resort, if persuasion fails, I believe that the attempt to retain our hold on congregations of Christians by merely financial bonds is unworthy and futile.

the whole community if improper persons are admitted or proper persons excluded. It is of vital importance that the Christians should learn to recognize this. It is possible to teach them and to help them to feel a proper responsibility in the matter. They will recognize the truth and feel the responsibility, if the truth is taught them and the responsibility is thrown upon them. No convert should be admitted by baptism into the body without the approval of the body, as a body. If a man wishes to be baptized he must be accepted by the congregation. But some one will say, 'If we do that, men will be rejected whom the missionary is convinced are proper persons'. If that is so, then the missionary must try to educate the congregation, but he will do that not by overruling them with a high hand, but by teaching them true principles. If the convert must go to the church, so must the missionary. He must entreat, exhort, advise with all long-suffering. He may fail to obtain his end in a particular case. But the people may be right and he be wrong. Even if he is right, he may really gain more by allowing the people to overrule him than by overruling them. They will speedily see that they are dealing with one who earnestly seeks their welfare, but will not force his own views upon them, and they will certainly be in greater danger of erring through their desire to please him than through their desire to vex him, or even to drive him away.

(c) *The appointment of ministers.* If a man is to be trained at a central school as a catechist or teacher, it is of the first importance that he should feel that he is sent by the whole community, not by the favouritism of a foreign missionary, that he is supported by the common assent and approval, that he represents the body, and that he will be received on his return by the whole body. No missionary is compelled to recommend in such cases on his sole authority. It is not enough that he should consult the Christians, he may see to it that the choice is the real choice of the whole congregation, or group of congregations, to which the candidate belongs. Beyond that the missionary cannot at the present time go. The appointment of catechists, deacons and priests to posts in the diocese is generally in the hands of the bishop or of a committee, and the people to whom the man is sent are seldom, if ever, consulted. So long as this is the case the missionary is compelled to accept the nominee of that committee, and the people can scarcely be expected to understand the true relations between the pastor and his flock. The situation is grievous; but in old-established missions it is at present unavoidable. For no one can expect a committee directed by foreigners to act on Pauline principles. The committee will inevitably make the bonds which bind the native ministers to itself as tight as possible, and the bonds which unite the minister to his flock proportionately weak. But if the missionary sees to it that no candidate is sent up from his district until he has really been selected and approved by the people to whom he naturally belongs he will lay a foundation upon which a better system may one day be established. At any rate, he will remove the common complaint that candidates for ordination and clergy are at the mercy of one man and that to displease the superintending missionary even accidentally is certain to result in the ruin of the man's career.

(d) *Discipline*. Cases of moral failure are more simple. In nearly every case the missionary in charge is left a very large discretion in such matters. He can act as St Paul acted. If a man falls into grievous sin, if an offence is committed which ought to shock the conscience of the whole Christian community, he need not deal with it directly. He can call the attention of the congregation to it and point out the dangers manifest and pressing of leaving it unrecognized or unreproved. He can call upon them to decide what ought to be done. He can in the last resort refuse to have any dealings with a congregation which declines to do its duty and tolerates gross open immorality in its midst. He can entreat, exhort, advise, he may even threaten, the whole body when it would be fatal to deal with the individual himself. If he can persuade them to do what is right, the whole community is uplifted; but he cannot put them in the right way by doing for them what they alone can do.[1]

(2) *He can train them for retirement by retiring.* He can retire in two ways, physically or morally. He can retire morally by leaving things more and more in their hands, by avoiding to press his opinion, by refusing to give it lest he should, as is often the case, lead them to accept his opinion simply because it is his. He can retire by educating them to understand all the working of the mission and by gradually delegating it. He can retire physically. He can go away on missionary

---

[1] A missionary in South Africa told me that he had practised the theory of discipline which he first found in this book, and that the result had surprised him. 'For the first time,' he said, 'I felt that we got to the root of the matter and justice was being done.'

tours of longer and longer duration, leaving the whole work of the station to be carried on without any foreign direction for a month or two. He can do this openly and advisedly because he trusts his people. He can prolong his tours. He can find excuses for being away more and more. He can even create such a state of affairs that he may take his furlough without their suffering any harm. At first, no doubt, he would be anxious, and he would have good cause for anxiety. Things would go wrong. But his people would know his mind, and, though they would grudge his absence, they would see that he was really helping them most by leaving them. Retirement of that kind, deliberately prepared and consciously practised, is a very different thing from absence through stress of business unwillingly. Only by retirement can he prepare the way for real independence.

But the difficulty instantly arises that in many cases the retirement of the missionary would mean that the Christians would be deprived of the sacraments. That is too often true, and it is apparently an insuperable difficulty. The only way out of it is to persuade the Bishop to ordain men in every place to celebrate the sacraments. There are plenty of suitable men. Everywhere there are good, honest, sober, grave men respected by their fellows, capable of this office, and they ought to be ordained for that special purpose. But meanwhile, even at the risk of depriving the Christians at the centre of that spiritual food which is their right, the missionary should retire, at any rate for a few months, in order to evangelize new districts, and above all to teach his people to stand alone.

But in every district the missionary has not only to deal with settled congregations. If he is an evangelist he is always beginning work in new towns or villages with new converts. Then he can begin at the very beginning. He can make the rule of practice the rule of all his teaching. Wherever he finds a small community of hearers he can begin by teaching them one simple truth, one prayer, one brief article of the Creed and leaving them to practise it. If on his return he finds that they have learned and practised that first lesson, he can then teach them a little more; but if he finds that they have not succeeded, he can only repeat the first lesson and go away again so that they may master that one before they are burdened with another. If they learn to practise one act alone they may make more progress than if they had learned by heart all the doctrines of the Church and depended solely upon some outside teacher. He need not take it for granted that, if men are converted, there is no hope for the conversion of their wives and children until he can get women missionaries and teachers to instruct them in the rudiments of the Gospel. He can tell his first converts that they are responsible not only for their own progress, but for the enlightenment of their wives and families and neighbours. In some places the difficulties of this are apparently insuperable; but men overcome apparently insuperable difficulties by the power of the Holy Ghost. We need not take it for granted that men or women must run away from home, or cannot influence their households and teach them what they have learned. It is better to take it for granted that they can, even to the death. Slaves in heathen households in Rome were in apparently an impossible position; yet they overcame the apparent impossibility.

He need not take it for granted that every small community of hearers must have a catechist settled amongst them. Where there are three people one will inevitably lead. On his visits the missionary, or his catechist, can give special attention and teaching to these natural leaders and instruct them to hand on to the others the special teaching which they have received. This can be done if the instruction given is given line upon line, and if there is no haste to complete a theological education. So these leaders will grow with their fellows, with those whom they teach. They will learn more by teaching than in any other way. If the missionary is fortunate he may be able to induce his bishop to ordain some of these men of approved moral character and natural authority. In that case the church in that part will grow naturally into completion: otherwise, his converts will be compelled to wait for his visits to receive the sacraments, the work will be retarded, and the people starved. But even so, he can make them largely independent in all other respects. The visits of the missionary will be welcomed as the visits of a friend who can help them. They will eagerly seek his advice, they will need his encouragement. But *whatever they have learnt, they will have so learnt that they can practise it, even if he never came near them again.* It would be better to teach a few men to call upon the name of the Lord for themselves than to fill a church with people who have given up idolatry, slavishly and unintelligently, and have acquired a habit of thinking that it is the duty of converts to sit and be taught, and to hear prayers read for them in the church by a paid mission agent. The missionary can observe the rule that no organization should be introduced which the people cannot understand and maintain. He need not begin by establishing buildings, he need not begin by importing foreign books and foreign ornaments of worship. The people can begin as they can with what they have. As they feel the need of organization and external conveniences they will begin to seek about for some way of providing them. The missionary, or his helper, can encourage and assist them. They may even subscribe money, but if they do this, it should be a subscription from them, freely given, and entirely in the control of the little congregation. Their finance so far as they have any common finance may be entirely in their own hands. It will obviously be small, and because it is small it is of great importance that they should learn to manage it themselves, so that they may be prepared to understand the larger finance of a wider area when they begin to find their place in an organization which covers a large district.

Similarly with all church rules, it is not necessary to begin by insisting upon mere verbal assent to a code of law. The new converts may grow up into it. If they learn to pray in twos and threes, if they learn to read as they may be able the Holy Gospels,[1] and to discuss amongst themselves the lessons of the teacher they will gradually perceive the inconsistency of that which they read or hear with heathen practices to which they have been accustomed. They will inquire amongst themselves and dispute; they will refer the question to the missionary on his visit and he will have opportunity of explaining wherein the custom in question is agreeable or otherwise to the doctrine which they have been taught. But he need not hurry them. They must learn to change because they feel the need of change, and to change because they see the rightness of the change, rather than to change because they are told to do so. If they change unintelligently, by order, they will easily relapse, because they have never seen the principle on which the change is based. Artificial changes are not likely to be permanent until they have become in process of years habitual, and then they will still be unintelligent. Changes made under the influence of the Holy Spirit are reasonable, and, so

---

[1] I have seen converts of the lowest castes in India after one year's teaching capable of reading and understanding the Gospels and doing the work of lay evangelists most efficiently.

made, are the accepted changes of the people themselves. From those they can only fall away by deliberate apostasy. So we advance at home. We educate public opinion until that opinion is on the side of righteousness and then the change is permanent. So, e.g., we put down slavery. And so we may deal with our converts.

Our past efforts have not been so fruitless but that we have now a great number of Christians who, beginning by accepting Christian law as an external demand of the foreign teachers, have ended by seeing its true meaning and accepting it as a proper expression of the will of God and here we have a powerful influence and example. New converts will speedily strive to attain the level of their fellows. They will see the manifest advantages. By setting the example before them of Christian communities more advanced than themselves, by encouraging them to take their difficutlies to their more educated brethren, we can encourage and help them without enforcing authoritative, and to them incomprehensible, demands.[1] Some things they will speedily accept because they are true and natural expressions of the mind of Christ in them; some things they will accept only after a long struggle, because they are not easily understood; and some things they will never accept because they are neither natural nor proper expressions of the mind of Christ in their lives; and such things have never been really accepted, even by those who have outwardly submitted to them.

But there would certainly arise cases in which the people would for a long time observe practices which the missionary would be compelled to condemn as superstitious, immoral, or otherwise iniquitous. Still the true method is purely persuasive. The missionary must use his judgment as to whether the refusal is deliberate rejection of a truth which the people know to be truth and will not accept, or whether it is due to ignorance and immature ideas of the nature of Christianity. In the latter case he can go on teaching, exhorting, persuading, certain that so far as he is right, he will lead the people to see that he is right. In the former case, he has no resort but to shake off the dust of his feet, to refuse to teach men who will not be taught. Compulsion is futile, and disastrous. There are men who will be taught. He must seek out those and turn to them.

This applies to all missionary preaching. The one test which the missionary should require of his hearers is openness of mind. If he

[1] The law as regards marriage is a noteworthy example of this.

teaches, he teaches as one who is making a moral demand, and if that moral demand is met with a flat determination to resist it, then he cannot well continue his teaching. Willingness to send children to school in order to obtain material advantage, if coupled with a determination not to submit to the claims of Christ, is not a field in which the doctrine of Christ can be planted. Willingness to listen to the preacher in order to rise in the social scale by becoming Christian is very different. There is a willingness to accept the teaching. The motive is low, but the willingness to accept is present, and the teacher can there plant seeds which will grow up and purify the motive. This has happened again and again. Willingness to hear for the sake of advantage with a determination not to submit to the doctrine is one thing, willingness to hear for the sake of advantage with even a half-hearted intention of accepting the doctrine is another. There must be in the hearers a willingness, not only to hear but to accept, if the missionary is to persevere with success. Everywhere there are those whose hearts God touches and so bring prepared hearts. On those the missionary may concentrate his attention. For them there is hope. Everywhere there are those who refuse to hear with their souls, who close their hearts. These we must prepare to refuse to teach. We must be prepared to shake the lap.

So far, any missionary who chooses can go today, without upsetting the work of his predecessors, but building upon it. Many things may seem desirable, but this at least is possible.

3

Epilogue

A Present-day Contrast

It may perhaps add point and reality to the argument which I have tried to set forth in the preceding pages, if I illustrate it by examples taken from modern life. I have imagined two men working under fairly similar circumstances. I have first made a composite photograph. All the details are taken from life, but no one missionary supplied me with them all. The picture which results is consequently imaginary; but it will, I think, be at once recognized as representing a real type, and that not an uncommon one. The second illustration is not composite. It is the actual experience of one actual man, and the story is extracted almost verbatim from his diary of his work.

I

The missionary was a good man, devoted to his work. He was sincerely desirous of building up the native church. He laboured in a large district and tried hard to do the work of two or three men.

He began by building schools and churches. He saw that unless the children of his converts received some education, they could not progress as he desired to see them progress. He saw that their parents were poor and could not afford to do very much to promote education; they could hardly afford to lose the help of their children even when they were young. Consequently he was driven to look elsewhere for support. He besought societies, he wrote letters, he enlisted the sympathies of his friends at home, he collected subscriptions. He exhorted and taught his converts until they began to understand that it was to their advantage to lend their help. Moreover they knew that he sought their welfare, and they were inclined to help him in any work which he started. So out of their poverty they subscribed money and labour, and in due course the schools were built—primary schools in the villages, and a high school at the central station. The schools were built on mission property and

23

belonged to the mission, and the mission supplied the teachers, and relied upon the teachers to keep up the interest of the church-folk in them and to induce them to send their children.

Similarly the missionary provided churches for his people. He said that if corporate church life was to be a reality the converts must have churches. These were provided in the same way and entailed no small labour and anxiety. In some cases he actually assisted at the building with his own hands: in all he exercised careful and consistent supervision. He was very anxious that his buildings should be as good and as church-like as possible, and not only in the exterior but in the internal fittings he strove to have everything not only good but attractive and complete. With the help of his friends in England he succeeded in providing some of them with bells and harmoniums. He introduced surpliced choirs, he induced guilds of ladies in England to send him out altar linen and frontals. He instructed his people in the use of the Prayer Book, and he managed by dint of persevering labour to teach them to conduct the service in good order. He even got them to sing translations of *Hymns Ancient and Modern*, for they were a musical people; though the tunes were to them unnatural and the translations imperfect and sometimes, to them, almost incomprehensible. Thus the services in his churches became the admiration of visitors from England.

Yet he was not quite satisfied. Churches and schools alike required perpetual supervision. There was a tendency amongst the converts to let things fall into decay the moment that his inspiring presence was withdrawn for a short time. The surplices were allowed to get dirty and ragged, the altar frontals became moth-eaten, the very fabric of the buildings was neglected. The people inclined sometimes to meet in informal services to sing native hymns which one of them had written to native tunes, to the neglect of the daily offices. The missionary was disheartened. He saw that it would take a long time to establish a habit of decent, orderly service, as he understood it. His converts had subscribed liberally, and he had boasted of their self-support. Yet they did not seem to look upon the fruits of their liberality as their own. They did not show any eager zeal to draw others from their heathen neighbours into the church.

Consequently he welcomed eagerly a diocesan scheme for the establishing of native church councils, because he hoped that, by this means, his people would learn to take a more intelligent and active part in the management of the church. He immediately set to work to carry out the new scheme. He directed his native pastors and helpers to see that the councils were elected. At first neither pastors nor people understood it. They saw in it simply a new method of getting money. One of the native pastors thus described his experience to a stranger: 'The people come to us and they say, "What does this mean? We do not want to be consulted. The missionaries are our father and our mother. Let the missionary tell us what to do and we will do it". And I say, "The missionaries have directed this. They want you to do this. They think it will educate you in the management of affairs and will make you more self-supporting. We must do it."' And they did. By degrees they began to find that it was interesting to be consulted, and they gained a new sense of importance. They not only subscribed money but within certain limits they administered it. It was true that the missionary audited all their accounts and objected strongly to any expenditure that he had not authorized, but, still, under his direction they did administer some funds. They also learnt to criticize the use of funds. They knew that much money came into the missionary's hands from mission sources, and they surmised that he administered more than they knew. They knew how much they themselves gave. They knew that the missionary boasted of their generosity. They, too, began to feel that they were doing a great deal. To strangers their first remark was a modest boast that they were far advanced in self-support, their second was a hint that they did not receive so much out of the mission funds as they thought that they had deserved.

They were not, of course, allowed to go far in self-government. The missionary felt that it would be extremely dangerous if people who had not learnt to walk were allowed to run. All their meetings were of the nature of instructions in what the missionary thought should be done, rather than free proposal and discussion. 'If they did what they liked, what should I do,' said the missionary, 'if they wanted to do something of which I did not approve? I must keep the direction of affairs in my own hands.' In this he was ably supported by his native pastors who were entirely independent of their congregations. The missionary wanted to appoint a special catechist to work amongst children—a sort of special missioner for children. In one pastorate the pastorate committee refused to see the wisdom or necessity of this; but the missionary had expressed a wish for it, and the pastor followed the missionary. The pastorate committee refused to support the plan, so the pastor vetoed their resolution. The district committee sitting under the chairmanship of the missionary accepted the plan. It was carried out. The pastorate committee thereupon passed a resolution to the effect that as the proposal had been carried over their heads and they disapproved of, it, they would not vote any money for its support. The pastor vetoed that resolution also, and paid the money out of the church fund, of which he was treasurer. Nevertheless, in spite of the fact that the committees did not always see eye to eye with their missionary, and consequently had to be overruled, their very existence did encourage the converts in self-support and did teach them the art of self-government to a certain degree. And the missionary was glad of that. He really wanted them to learn to manage their own affairs, only in the early stages he felt that it was of vital importance that they should not be allowed to go wrong.

Similarly in cases of discipline he was most anxious to educate the people. He did not believe in the exercise of discipline as the mere decree of white missionaries. He thought the people should be represented. In cases of serious wrong-doing, he caused a committee of inquiry to be appointed, and if the case presented any peculiar difficulty he himself went down and sat on the committee at the inquiry. No doubt justice was done. But it was disappointing to find that Christians often refused hospitality to a man who had been so excommunicated when the missionary was present, and then received him when the missionary was absent. They did not seem to realize the full responsibility of their action. If it was suggested that the case might have been different if the native body had acted in the first instance alone, the answer was conclusive: 'It would be dreadful if the Native Committee condoned a moral offence.'

Such was the missionary's energy and success in governing his native converts that he was appointed Secretary of the Diocesan Conference of his Mission. There he could exercise his abilities over a wider area. It was unfortunate that his knowledge of the language was not sufficient to enable him to write or translate papers quickly, because the rule of the Conference was that all business should be transacted in the native tongue; but the difficulty was got over by allowing the rule to lapse. Happily nearly all the native members of conference, or at any rate all the more influential members, could speak English, and speeches could be delivered on occasion in the vernacular for the benefit of those who could understand no other tongue. But here, too, the missionary and his fellows felt the necessity of keeping the conduct of affairs safe in their own hands. One day, one of his own people rose at the conference to propose that a certain building which had been originally put up as a residence for a foreign missionary should be converted into a secondary school for the people of that district. This was a proposal of which the missionary heartily disapproved. It struck directly at the position of the secondary school in his own central station which was under his own immediate care. He rose to oppose it. Nevertheless he could not convince the proposer, who again got up and began a long speech on behalf of his plan. He was very eager about it because he was himself a native of the place and a leading churchman there. Thereupon the missionary broke in and cut him short abruptly. His argument, this time was conclusive. 'Well, anyhow,' he said, 'it is *our* building, it is not *your* building, and we will not let you have it for the purpose.'

II

The second was in charge of a much smaller district. He began by approaching his bishop with a request that the usual grant given for the upkeep of his mission station might be withdrawn. He desired that his own salary and the salaries of his three native catechists might be paid them but no more. 'If,' he said, 'we need money for any purpose, we will apply for it, explaining what we can do, what we propose to do, and what help we need, and you, if you think good, can help us out of mission funds. I will see that the work is done, and will inform you when it is done. But I shall keep no mission accounts, for I shall never keep any mission money in my hands.'

At the direction of his bishop, and as part of a diocesan scheme, he caused a council to be elected by the four little churches in his district, and he used that council. If anything needed to be done in any of the churches, either the congregation found out the need for itself, or the missionary suggested the need until the congregation felt it. When they recognized the need, they met as a congregation to discuss it (if the missionary was present, he was present; if he was not, he was not), and to consider what they could do to supply it. If they could supply it, they did so without any further question, and when the missionary came round they displayed their work with pride and were duly congratulated. If they needed help, they instructed their representatives to go to the District Council to appeal for them. The representatives appeared at the council, and set forth the case, and said how much the local church could guarantee towards the expense and how much they needed.

The District Council had a small fund in the hands of its treasurer from which, if it approved of the scheme, it voted a grant. If that was not enough to supply the need, the missionary then reported the matter to the bishop: 'The local church wants *such and such* things done. It is prepared to subscribe *so much*; the District Council is prepared to subscribe *so much*; they still need *so much*. I think the local subscription is sufficient to justify the conclusion that the people really are in earnest about it (or are *not*, as the case might be). I think the District Council grant is sufficient to justify the conclusion that the council is agreed that the work ought (or ought *not*, as the case might be) to be done. Can you supply the deficiency?' If the money was given, it was handed over to the District Council, which then gave it with its own grant to the local church, and the work was done, and there an end.

At first this caused great amazement amongst the people. A local church wanted a school. The people appealed to the missionary and asked him to found one in their village. They said, 'We want a school'. 'Then why don't you get one?' was the answer. They were astonished. 'What?' they said, 'how can we get one?' 'How do your heathen neighbours get their children taught?' 'They subscribe together and invite a teacher.' 'Well, why don't you do that?' 'But that has never been done. The missionary has always found the teacher.' 'I cannot help that. I do not see why I should find your teachers. I have no teachers; you have. Is there not among you a single man who can teach a few little boys to read and write and say their catechism?' 'But *may we* do that?' 'Of course, why not?' 'But how shall we pay him?' 'Look here,' said the missionary, 'you go away and think it out and talk it over. See what you can do and then come and report to me, and perhaps I will give you a subscription out of my own pocket, if you are in difficulties.' (Here he made a mistake; he ought to have told them to report to the District Council: but it was his first case, and he had not himself thought things out.) So they went away, and in due course the school was begun. It cost the missionary about £1.

He said little about the Church, the Body, Unity; he always acted as if the Church, the Body, the Unity was a reality. He treated the church as a church. He declined to treat individual members of the body as mere individuals. Before he reached the district there had been grievous troubles and disturbances, great persecutions, and afflictions. In fear of their lives some of the Christians had fallen away. They did not indeed, so far as I know, practise heathen rites, but they did not come to church and they were unwilling to be openly associated with the Christian congregation. The missionary did not search out these people. He addressed himself to the church. He pointed out to the church the great danger in which these lapsed Christians were, and how serious were the evils which might result from their continued impenitence. He reminded the Christians that they formed the permanent element in the church, and that the good name of the church was of vital importance to them. He asked them what steps they proposed to take, and he left them to decide what they thought ought to be done. They appointed certain of their number to visit the lapsed Christians, in order to set before them the dangers of their state and to ask them to decide on which side they would stand: with the Church for Christ, or with the heathen. They sent out their representatives with prayer. They received their report with thanksgiving. In a few days most of the lapsed were restored to the church.

One case was of a more difficult character. In the height of the persecution a prominent member of the church had driven away his son's wife, and had contracted for him a marriage with the daughter of one of the leaders of the persecuting society. This had happened more than two years before the missionary arrived in the district. For two years the offence had been passed over in silence. The offender and his son were both still Christians in name. As soon as the missionary found this out he called the church together. Again he urged upon the Christians the grievous and palpable dangers of condoning such an offence. Again he left them to consider what ought to be done. After a time the catechist, and one or two other members of the church, came to tell him that the church was agreed that the offenders ought to be excommunicated publicly. To that he replied that it was not within the power of the local church to excommunicate any member. All that they could do was to forward their resolution to the bishop with the request that he would take action in the case. He said that he was quite willing to write to the bishop for the church in that sense. So he did. But in the meanwhile he met the offender and told him what the church was doing. The offender came to see him. He was much disturbed. 'Why,' he said, 'cannot you act as your predecessors have always acted? Before, if any one did anything wrong, the priest wrote a letter to the bishop, the bishop wrote a letter to the church, the letter was read out in church, the man stayed away, and after that no more was said about it. Why cannot you do that? Why do you stir up all the Christians in such matters?' The missionary answered that public notorious offences concerned not only the priest-in-charge and the bishop, but the whole church, and that it was right that the church should act in such cases as a body. 'But what can I do?' asked the man. 'I cannot bear this.' The missionary replied that he did not know, but that he thought that if the man was truly penitent, and made public confession in the church, and then published his confession in the city, so that the name of the church was cleared, then the Christians might be satisfied and that he might remain in the church as a penitent, until the Hand of God made clear the way for his full restoration. Thereupon the man departed. Afterwards the missionary met his catechist and told him what he had said, and asked him whether he thought the Christians would be satisfied with such an act of penitence. 'It is of no importance,' answered the catechist, 'what they think. Such a thing has never been done since the world began. Whatever he may do, he will not do that.' Yet he did. It is one thing to be excommunicated by a foreign bishop, it is quite another to be excommunicated by one's neighbours. The whole church was in a ferment. Many of the Christians were connected by family ties with the offenders. They took the matter seriously to heart. Prayers went up to God night and day from individuals and from the whole church. The offender read out in church a confession couched in the simplest and most definite terms. In it he confessed that he had committed such an offence, that his action was contrary to the laws of God and the Church, that he was persuaded that salvation was to be found in Christ in communion with His Church, and that thenceforward he would endeavour to conform his life to the Law of God. He went out with two or three of the leaders of the church and posted that confession on the four gates of the city.

Soon the missionary learnt that the secret of success in his work lay in dealing with the church as a body. When questions arose he had but one answer, 'Tell it to the church'. A man came to him one day with a long tale of persecution. His landmark, he said, had been removed by a heathen neighbour who, not content with robbing him, was accusing him of the very offence which he himself had committed. The injured Christian begged for assistance against his adversary. The only answer that he received was, 'Tell it to the church'. Eventually he did so. After service one Sunday morning, he rose and said, 'I have business for the church'. All gave him a patient hearing whilst he poured out his tale. Then an old farmer in the congregation rose and asked: 'Has your adversary taken the case into court?' 'No, but he threatens to do so.' 'Then I propose that we adjourn this matter until he carries out his threat.' Not another word was said. Some weeks later the same man came to say that his enemy had now taken the case into court and to appeal for help. Again, an old man arose: 'I think that we had better not consider this matter any more.' Again the sentence was received in silence. In that silence the whole church had condemned their brother. They held him to be in the wrong. A question which might have perplexed and troubled a foreigner, one in which he might easily have made a serious mistake, was settled. No Christian in the congregation would have dared to tell a foreign priest that the man was wrong. None would have dared to advise him not to give his countenance to another. But none was ready to uphold the evil himself, none need break that silence of condemnation. They all knew every detail of the case, details which none would have ventured to utter even in private. The aged, respectable leader, illiterate, ignorant in many ways, dull though he might be, in the council of the church found his voice and fulfilled a duty which would have tried the wisdom of the best educated and best instructed teacher.

Very soon the church began to realize itself. Sunday after Sunday the congregation sat discussing questions of church order, or instructing one another in the faith. Most often the missionary could not himself be present, and often when he might have been present, he felt that it was wise to leave his people to thresh out their questions and difficulties in their own way, and to report to him their decisions, or to send their questions to him, if they wanted his advice. He was not afraid that they would make serious mistakes or take hasty action behind his back. The more he retired from them, the more they turned to him in case of need, the more they sought his advice, the more they told him their plans, the more they saved him from difficulties. One day, on his return from an outlying village, he was met by his catechist with the familiar question: 'Do you know what we have been doing today?' 'No. What have you been doing?' 'We have adopted a baby.' The children of a poor Christian playing in the fields had heard a cry. Seeing no one near, they searched about till they discovered a box lightly covered with soil, from which the cry came. They broke it open and found a young baby. They took it home to their father. He, poor man, was utterly unable to satisfy another mouth. So next Sunday he went to church and told his tale. Thereupon the Christians decided to give it into the care of one of their number and to pay her a weekly dole for its maintenance. It was baptized with a name which in English means 'one who has obtained love'. When the missionary heard this he was glad. If he had not taught the people to 'Tell it to the church', the baby might have been put down on his doorstep, and he might have been driven to begin the foundation of a costly 'Foundlings' Home'. But happily for him, the church had learnt to manage its own business.

Sometimes it was his part to suggest the doing of charity. One day the catechist told him that the husband of a poor woman was dead, and the family was hard put to it to arrange the funeral. 'Get *so and so* to bring the case before the church.' After the meeting the missionary asked the catechist what the church had done. The church had subscribed *so much*. 'Is that enough?' 'Barely.' Then the missionary, too, as a member of the church, could subscribe. He was not outside the church. He could act with the church, but not instead of, or without it.

All this may sound very trivial. But yet it led the catechist to see the hope of a native church before him as a reality more clearly than all the teaching which he had received. And he learnt that lesson in three months. All the matters recorded here happened in less than six months, and he and many others had grasped the truth of the situation long before the end of that time. One day he came into the missionary's house with a question. 'Do you know what you are doing, sir?' 'Yes,' answered the missionary, 'I think that I know; but I should like to know what you think I am doing.' 'Well, sir, if you go on like this you will found a native church.'

The Way of Spontaneous Expansion

Editorial Note

Allen begins *The Spontaneous Expansion of the Church* by relating how he came to his fundamental position, stating broadly the danger he saw and its remedy. Allen argues in chapter 2 that spontaneous expression on the part both of individuals and churches is the key to expansion and that the restriction of this spontaneous expression, from fear of its uncontrollable character, though natural, is disastrous. In the next chapter Allen compares two theories of missions and, rejecting the theory which aims at the establishment of a Church by a process of devolution, examines other, then recent, efforts (such as those of Bishop Tucker in Uganda) to follow a practice more in harmony with the practice of the apostolic age; he also shows where such efforts fall short. Allen begins in chapter 4 to examine the fears which hinder us from following the apostolic practice, focusing especially on the fear that we might not be able to maintain our standard of *doctrine*. Allen argues here that our conception of the standard of doctrine is false, as is our method of maintaining it; and our fears put a serious barrier in the way of progress. In the next chapter he examines the Christian standard of *morals* and argues that the standard we try to enforce is something less than the Christian standard. Our attempt to enforce that standard presents the Gospel as a system of law and undoes the victory of St Paul over the Judaizing party which opened the door to the expansion of the Church in the West. Chapter 6 is entitled 'Civilization and Enlightenment.' Allen contends that we put the cart before the horse, or the fruit before the tree which should bear the fruit — instead of establishing the Church and then assisting in its education, we insist that the education and the civilization must come before the establishment of the Church. Allen argues in chapters 7 and 8 that our mission societies and boards make progress dependent upon money and foster a system of 'mission by proxy' that is the antithesis of spontaneous expansion. He further contends that our ecclesiastical system and our conception of ministerial training contrast sharply with the simplicity and directness of the apostolic method — the way of spontaneous expansion.

4

The rapid and wide expansion of the Church in the early centuries was due in the first place mainly to the spontaneous activity of individuals. As I pointed out in my first chapter, a natural instinct to share with others a new-found joy, strengthened and enlightened by the divine Grace of Christ, the Saviour, inevitably tends to impel men to propagate the Gospel. The early Church recognized this natural instinct and this divine Grace, and gave free scope to it. Very many of the Christians in those local churches had no doubt become Christians, led by the spontaneous zeal of someone who was a Christian before them. The names of a few great apostles were known to the whole Church; but the first teachers of the majority of the Christians were probably unknown to any but those whom they had quietly influenced. No one, then, was surprised at the spontaneous efforts of individual Christians to convert others to their Faith. They probably thought it quite natural. Thus as men moved about there were constantly springing up new groups of Christians in different places.

The Church expanded simply by organizing these little groups as they were converted, handing on to them the organization which she had received from her first founders. It was itself a unity composed of a multitude of little churches any one of which could propagate itself, and consequently the reception of any new group of Christians was a very simple matter. By a simple act the new group was brought into the unity of the Church, and equipped, as its predecessors had been equipped, not only with all the spiritual power and authority necessary for its own life as an organized unit, but also with all the authority needed to repeat the same process whenever one of its members might convert men in any new village or town. Thus the results of the spontaneous labour of any individual Christian were naturally and easily consolidated and established within the unity of the Church.

I

This spontaneous activity of the individual, rooted as it is in a universal instinct, and in a Grace of the Holy Spirit given to all Christians, is not peculiar to any one age or race. We are familiar with it today. It constantly shows itself, and it would repeat the history of the early Church, if it were not that our fears have set up barriers in the way of its proper fruition, as I have attempted to show in earlier chapters. What we see today is the spontaneous zeal of Christians attempting to repeat, so far as they can, the early history of the Christian Church. The only reason why such spontaneous activity on the part of our converts has not resulted in the foundation of churches, is because our bishops have treated them in a very different way from that in which the bishops of the early centuries treated those who did precisely the same work. They equipped them and set them free; we have refused to equip them, and have bound them to the foreign organization of our mission. Thus we have cast down the men whose spontaneous zeal led them to convert their neighbours and friends by setting over them our trained and paid lay catechists; thus we have discouraged any others who might have followed their example. We have looked upon such spontaneous activity as something strange and wonderful. When we find an example of it told in our missionary magazines we generally find it associated with notes of exclamation and expressions of astonishment or anxiety. We have not known how to expect it, we have not known how to deal with it, and consequently it is not unnaturally more rare than it ought to be. Still it remains so essentially the natural action of that instinct to impart a joy, and that gift of the Holy Spirit who is the Spirit which desires and strives after the salvation of men, that in spite of our discouragement it constantly breaks out afresh. I have already had occasion to refer to some examples, I will here only cite two more as typical of a larger number.

(1) An African priest in charge of the mission at Tarquah on the Gold Coast gives the following account of one of his experiences:

I was called to visit some Christians at a village 163 miles from my station. . . . When I arrived I met about a hundred converts waiting for baptism. A young man from one of our stations, who has no teacher, had managed to learn to read a little of the New Testament and the Prayer Book in Fanti. He went up to this village, where some of his relations

35

lived, early in 1920. There he started teaching his own people, and the good news spread. They built a little church and for a year he laboured hard, teaching them as much as he could every morning before they went to their farms, and in the evening before they retired to rest. When he thought that they were ready for baptism, he heard of our scarcity of clergy and encouraged them to wait. After careful examination on my arrival I baptized forty-five adults.[1]

(2) Last month I had the Rev. Fong Hau Kong here for three weeks, to assist me by visiting some of my Chinese congregations. I sent him to Tuaran, about twenty-two miles from here, where there was a congregation that had never been visited by a clergyman since its settlement in the country. I had received an invitation to go to them, but I thought it better to send Mr Fong, as I have no knowledge of Chinese. He found a congregation of over forty Christians who had come from China nearly ten years ago, and settled as gardeners. They had elected as their teacher and reader one of their party, a man named Chang Shu Chung. He had in his early days been a teacher of a heathen school, but was converted to Christianity, and subsequently became a teacher in a mission school at Foo Chow. At first the community subscribed to pay a salary to their teacher, but later they were not so prosperous, and the salary ceased. Chang Shu Chung has, however, gone on with his work without any pay, and Sunday after Sunday has not failed to assemble the people for worship in the little church which they built for themselves. On the Sunday that Mr Fong spent with them he had a congregation of over forty, and administered Holy Communion to fourteen, and Baptism to one adult and eleven infants. This was the first occasion since they left China that they had been visited by a priest, or had an opportunity of receiving the sacraments.[2]

We see in both these cases a spontaneous expansion of the Church so far as these people were able: we see what might have been churches founded without any assistance, or direction, from the foreign missionaries. These people were self-supporting: they received no grants of any description from any society, they were able to supply all their own needs: they had built their own churches and they maintained their own services. Their leader was exercising what in an earlier age would have been called a charismatic ministry. They were self-governing, directing all the affairs of their own church. All that was needed for their establishment was that their leaders should have been ordained; for in both cases they had evidently been taught, or at any rate had somehow learned, that

[1] *World Wide Witness*, SPG Report for 1921, p. 84.
[2] *Borneo Miss. Chron.*, Aug. 1911.

only ordained men could baptize or administer the Lord's Supper. If this difficulty had been removed by Ordination, then in each case we should have seen at once the creation of a new church on truly apostolic lines, and the example so set would certainly have encouraged and inspired other native Christians to have followed the example set them.

Churches so founded would have been unquestionably native churches. The least intelligent native looking at them must at once have perceived that here was something which it needed no foreigner to maintain. They would have been native churches in a very different sense from those pseudo-national native churches which we talk about creating. Such churches would bring new life into the mission field, and open all the doors closed to us. The existence of one prophesies the conversion of the country. As I said before, these cases are not rare: almost every country in the world can show similar examples, and in some parts of the world they are quite common. The Bishop of Lagos, for instance, has told us that in Southern Nigeria the greatest progress of recent years has been due not so much to the direct work of the European missionaries, or of paid African teachers, as to the spontaneous work of untrained and unpaid native Christians.[1]

I believe the time is ripe for this advance. I have already tried to show that our present missions are not the natural homes of spontaneous expansion; but the societies themselves are doing something to prepare the way. They are now tending to concentrate more and more upon medical, educational and social work carried on in institutions; and as they do that, their resources in men and money will be so fully occupied that they must inevitably withdraw more and more from direct evangelistic work, and look upon this work as the proper work of native Christians; and many of our evangelistic missionaries are certainly looking in this direction. There is, therefore, a good hope that a movement towards spontaneous expansion may arrive at a propitious moment.

II

Let us suppose then that a missionary hears of such a case as one of those which I have quoted, or himself by his preaching has prepared a small body of men for baptism. Let us suppose that some of them

[1] CMS *Gleaner*, April 1921, p. 69.

have been baptized. We must realize that baptized Christians have rights. What are those rights? They have a right to live as Christians in an organized Christian Church where the sacraments of Christ are observed. They have a right to obey Christ's commands, and to receive His Grace. In other words they have a right to be properly organized with their own proper ministers. They have a right to be a church, and not a mere congregation. These are the inalienable rights of Christians, and we cannot baptize people and then deny their rights, or deprive them of them. When we baptize we take responsibility for seeing that those whom we baptize can so live in the church.

What then ought the missionary to do? If he has baptized the first converts we may take it for granted that he has assured himself that they are in the Faith, and he ought then to invite the bishop to act towards them as the apostles and their immediate followers acted in like case. The little group must be fully equipped with spiritual power and authority; and the bishop ought to deliver to them the Creed, the Gospel, the Sacraments and the Ministry by solemn and deliberate act. It is to do that work that we have missionary bishops.

(1) The bishop must deliver to them what St Paul called 'the tradition' (of which the Apostles' Creed is the later expression) that they may have a standard by which to try all that they may hear later. The Creed is a touchstone. It is by that that they will know whether any teaching they may hear is to be received or to be rejected. It does not follow that every member of that little church must know by heart a form of words as long as the Apostles' Creed; but it does follow that when each has heard it (and it may be expressed in very simple language so that the most ignorant can really *hear* it), he must be prepared to say, 'That I believe: That is my belief.' It is in this sense that the Creed is to be delivered to the church. Thereafter it is theirs. It belongs to them as much as it belongs to us.

(2) The bishop must deliver to them the Gospel, that they may know where to turn for instruction. For they must learn from the very beginning to rely upon God, not upon men, for spiritual progress; upon the Bible, not upon human teachers, for spiritual instruction. Here again, when he delivers the Bible to the church, it does not follow that every member in the congregation must be able to read it; but it does follow that all the Christians must learn

to revere it, and to know it. Consequently in such churches every possible mark of honour should be attached to the power to read and explain the Bible. Double honour to those who labour in the word and doctrine. The priest in such a church is not necessarily the preacher. The Bible is read by those best able to read it and expound it; but no man's mouth should be closed, and the most illiterate will sometimes be found able to make a comment of the most profound spiritual significance because it is rooted in his experience.

A writer is quoted in the *International Review of Missions* for October 1920,[1] as saying:

> A village panchayat may be an assembly of illiterate men, but it is not an assembly of ignorant men, by any means. Nor are they men uneducated in matters of government. Indian villagers, even pariah villages, have had centuries of education in matters of government and administration. It is often because our missionaries do not know enough of the vernacular really to follow an Indian palaver that they fail to discover how much sound sense and clear reasoning and practical wisdom there is in it.

And the same truth applies to the church. Illiterate members often bring to the church a profound spiritual knowledge, and a sense of the practical application of Christian truth to daily life, which is hidden from the accomplished student. This then is what I mean by the delivery of the Gospel to the church. The Bible is delivered to the whole Church as the message of God to the whole Church. Thenceforward it belongs to them and is in their care. It is theirs as much as it is ours.

(3) The sacraments must be delivered to the church. The bishop must make sure that they have learnt the manner and the meaning of their observance. They must be taught how to administer them, and how to receive them, practically. They must not be allowed to think, as some of them may have gathered from their observation of a mission station, that baptism is the end of a long probation during which a man has proved his capacity to observe Christian laws; but they must think of it as the beginning of a Christian life which a man cannot live without God's Grace. They must be taught how to administer it, and if necessary they must be warned of the grave dangers which may ensue if they abuse its use, dangers from which the whole congregation, and the whole Christian Church may suffer. They must be taught how to administer the Holy Communion, and how to re-

[1] p. 560.

ceive it, and that in a very practical way. They must be taught the meaning of the Holy Communion, and here I am very bold. I have a profound belief in the power of the sacraments. I believe that in a divine way the use of them teaches the teachable their inward meaning so that the Church grows by degrees into a deeper and deeper sense of the divine Grace imparted in them; and therefore I think that we need be in no hurry to attempt to teach new converts all that we think we know about them. I think it suffices if we begin with some one aspect of the Holy Communion, and that the one which our converts can most easily apprehend, whether the Common Meal at which Christ is the Host, or the Common Sacrifice which all offer together, or the Common Thanksgiving for the Common Salvation through the death of Christ. If they learn one of these in its simplest form, they can learn the others by degrees. Much they will learn without any teaching from others, by their reading of the Bible in common, much from participation; for in the common rite they will find in experience a common bond between Christian and Christian, and of all with Christ. And by degrees they will discover the profound significance of such Communion with one another and with Christ. Thus the first teaching need not be long or difficult of apprehension. This is what I mean by the delivery of the sacraments to the Church: they should be delivered to the Church as a whole; and the Church as a whole should be responsible for their proper observance. When the Corinthians misused the Lord's Supper, St Paul rebuked the whole Church.

(4) Ministers must be ordained that the church may have a Christian government and officers to direct the proper conduct of the church and the due administration of her rites.

The selection of these officers should not be difficult. St Paul in the pastoral epistles has laid down, very clearly, rules to guide a bishop in the selection of such officers. They were to be, he said, men of good moral character, free from the besetting vices of their people, men of experience and weight, men held in the highest respect by the members of the church and their heathen neighbours, men who knew the tradition and could uphold it, men who could maintain order by their moral superiority; in fact the men whom any decent society would naturally choose for its leaders. To these men must be delivered the authority to administer the sacraments and to guide and govern the church in its religious services and its daily social life. No question of pay should be raised or considered. St Paul did not raise it: we need not.

But here again it is the Church as a whole which receives officers, not officers which receive a Church. Ministers should be given to a church, not a church to a minister, and the Church as a whole should be responsible for the good conduct of its officers, just as the officers are responsible for the good conduct of the Church. When a member of the church at Corinth committed a moral offence St Paul did not rebuke the elders of the church only, he rebuked the Church as a whole. A church thus constituted is a real church in the apostolic sense of the word.

(5) There is one other point which I think the bishop should impress upon the church if he is seeking for spontaneous expansion. It is not that he should exhort them to take the Gospel to their neighbours; but that he should tell them what to do when they have made converts in their neighbourhood too remote to be intimately attached to their own body, or in case people from a neighbouring village came to them to learn the Christian Faith. He should tell them first to make sure that the new converts are really converts to the faith of Christ and understand the *use* of the Creed, the Gospels, the Sacraments and the Ministry, and then to send word to the bishop.

III

Having done this the missionary and the bishop should leave that newly constituted church to find out for itself what being a church means in daily practice, to find out that it can do things as a church. When I say that he must leave such a church to find out for itself what a church is, I do not mean that he should neglect it; for he ought to take thought for its education. We must learn the distinction between leaving Christians to learn what they can only learn for themselves, and abandoning them. It is a distinction which we find it hard to make; it is a lesson which we find it hard to learn. The moment any one suggests leaving new converts to find out for themselves by their experience without the guidance of a foreign missionary how to manage the simple affairs of a simple village church, instantly the father-mother, elder-brother, directing, spirit of the energetic missionary rises in revolt and cries: 'You cannot abandon them so early to their own devices.' To leave new-born churches to learn by experience is apostolic, to abandon them is not apostolic: to watch over them is apostolic, to be always nursing them is not apostolic: to guide their education is apostolic, to provide it for them is not apostolic. The missionary and the bishop must watch over their education.

Instantly we perceive that the education of which we are speaking is something very different from what is commonly called missionary education. Missionary education, commonly so called, is a thing of schools and colleges, and for the few. The education of which we are now speaking is the education of the church and embraces the whole Christian community. The education of which we are speaking is education in the church, of the church and by the church.

It is essentially religious education, not in the sense in which we talk of religious education in schools where religious education means instruction in the subject-matter of the religion, given by a teacher for an hour in a day which is devoted mainly to secular education, but in a very different sense. This is an eductaion in the management and direction of the Christian church as a body, and of the family as a Christian family. The religious life is the one subject, and there is no other. The one thing to be learned is how to live the Christian life in that state and social order in which the Christians find themselves.

It is an education which Europeans cannot conduct because few, if any, Europeans can ever really understand the position of new converts from heathenism: they cannot look at the position from the inside; and it can only be the fruit of an internal growth. But if they cannot conduct it, they can watch over it, and they can assist it, as well as retard it. The education of the church is rather to be compared to the education of an infant in the use of its faculties than to the education of a boy in the Latin grammar. A good master can teach a boy Latin grammar. It is in a very different sense that a mother teaches a child to walk, or to see and to observe. Nature will teach the majority of children to walk, if they are allowed the use of their limbs. So the church learns the use of its faculties if it is allowed the use of its faculties.

The man then who would guide such a church as I have described and assist its education must obviously get out of the way to give it room; because if he stays, or if he leaves some one from outside in charge, it will plainly not have room to move. But he must watch over it and warn it by instruction when it is in danger of going seriously astray, or of falling heavily. The exact point at which such warning is necessary is a question of the most intimate delicacy; and it can only be solved by the instinct and insight of the educator with the watchful eye. It is impossible for any one else to judge, or to lay down any rule beforehand.

This practical education of the church I have put first, because it is the most important and the most fundamental education. The church must learn to use its faculties, and it can only do that by using them.

In doing this it will by itself both reveal and train the leaders of the future. By exercising government in the small body, the real leaders of the church learn to govern and direct a church composed of many such little churches. By teaching in the small body they learn to instruct a church composed of many such churches. By active evangelistic work in their own neighbourhood they learn to lead a mission in a whole province.

I said that the education was wholly religious. It is an education in how to apply the Christian faith to life under the conditions in which the Christians live. That is the one thing which matters, and that cannot be learnt in a school, but only in the world of life. Nevertheless there are certain aids which do materially assist the student of that art. I said that the one thing needful was to learn to apply the Christian Faith to life, and obviously to that end the study of the Bible is all important. When I spoke of the church, I took it for granted that at least one member of the congregation could read the Bible, and that there was a Bible or at least a Gospel in their language. That is not perhaps absolutely necessary; for the tradition might be handed down orally, and a church might make immense progress though all its members were illiterate. Nevertheless it is obvious that knowledge of the Bible is of great importance. Generally speaking it is true that most of those earnest Christians who have spontaneously taught their friends and neighbours have received some instruction, and have learnt to read, and can, therefore, teach someone else to read. But if we suppose an absolutely illiterate community we should all agree that a man watchful of the education of the churches would desire that they should be able to have the Bible read to them, and would take steps to secure this as far as he could.

There are two ways in which that can be done; for I exclude of course the sending of a paid mission teacher to live in the place and to do for the church everything that it ought to do for itself. The church can either invite someone who is able to read to teach a few of its own members to read, or it can send one or two of its members, or some of its members can go of their own free motion, to learn this art elsewhere. Neither of these courses is difficult, provided that the Christians have learned what is the place of the Bible in the church. If they have learned to pay it due honour they will respect and admire those who have knowledge of it, and out of it can show them larger and truer conceptions of Christian doctrine. There is no need to insist upon this. Muslims travel from Nigeria to Cairo to learn the Koran. Men universally respect the man who possesses in larger measure than they do themselves knowledge of a subject which they feel to be of vital importance; and no one need have any anxiety that this rule will not apply.

From the point of view of spontaneous expansion, we have no need to think of secular education, as we call it, at all, nor to make any provision for it. It is quite certain that men who learned to read religiously for a strictly religious purpose would certainly in some cases begin to desire and to win for themselves and their children further education in what we call secular subjects. If there were no mission schools, they would still do it, by using government schools if there were any such; and if there were none they would in time create schools for themselves. Given any opportunity at all, it is quite certain that intellectual enlightenment would increase in a church which was the home of religious teaching. And such enlightenment beginning in spiritual illumination would be well founded, and the church would remain always a fountain of enlightenment. The whole church would grow together in enlightenment, as each member brought in a new contribution, and each generation made some advance.

To us progress might seem slow; but all true educationalists know well the importance of slow growth for solid progress, even in the education of the individual; and when we are dealing with the education of a community we are thinking in terms not of years but of generations, and we must learn not to despise slow growth. The one thing of importance is that there should be some growth, some progress, however slight it may be in the eyes of the casual observer.

This then is what I mean by watching over the education of the church. To some minds this may seem inadequate, and they may think that we should make better progress by exercising direct control and forcing the pace. But I hope I have given reason to think that this is not really true, when we consider that we are building for the centuries; and at any rate I hope that no one will now accuse me of advocating the abandonment of our converts to their own devices; for surely all that I have been saying is the direct opposite of abandonment. To watch and to assist spontaneous progress is certainly not to abandon converts to their own devices.

IV

The question may be asked; for it is nearly always the first question asked when any reform is proposed: How would you apply that to congregations which have learned from the very beginning to rely upon foreign support and guidance? Now it is plain that to ordain simple unpaid villagers and to constitute a church among them is quite a different thing from ordaining paid and trained mission agents. There may be, there are, among these paid agents men who, because they really have become the trusted leaders of their people, would continue to lead them, if they and the people whom they lead were free; but in many cases, if the people were free to choose, and the paid catechists had not the support of the foreigners behind them, the leaders whom we set to lead would not lead for another day. If we removed the pay and the support of our authority, the Christians would revert tomorrow to the guidance of their old and experienced fathers, and leave these trained native agents on one side. With such material it is impossible to constitute the church. It is a sad thing, but it is nevertheless true, that if we talk of establishing the local church, the very men who have trained leaders for the native church, cry out that those men whom they have trained are not fit for this purpose. Neither these foreign teachers nor these native teachers, nor the congregations led and directed by them are prepared. Here and there the bishop might find cases in which it would be possible to constitute the church at once; and perhaps those cases are really more numerous than I imagine. But however that may be, I myself look for the salvation of these pauperized communities rather through the influence which the sight of young churches advancing spontaneously in the freedom of the Gospel will exercise upon them than by any direct action or exhortation on our part; because I am sure that properly constituted churches would expand as they felt and knew their power.

The way to convert the older missions is to show them what spontaneous expansion means in practice. As I have said spontaneous expansion is spontaneous. It is not created by exhortation. It springs up unbidden. Where men see it they covet it, and when the converts of the older missions see it they will begin to desire it. Desiring it, they will begin to seek it, and in seeking it to express it. Meanwhile they continue as they are. The missionary of spontaneous expansion need not be over-anxious about them. He need not hasten to convert them. He can leave them to their present foreign leaders with perfect confidence, assured that they too will awaken when the time is ripe.[1] He will not lack room for his work because of their existence, for they never have, and never will, occupy all the land.

v

But some one may say:

> The expansion of the early Church was, according to your own statement, due in large measure to the fact that in the early church bishops were consecrated for the new churches who could in their turn consecrate others for any new churches which might spring up in their neighbourhood; but you asked for no more than the ordination of priests in the village churches, and they could not ordain priests for churches which might spring up in their neighbourhood. If you want to return to the practice of the early Church, why do you not have the courage of your opinions, and ask that bishops should be again consecrated for the village, and town, churches; so that they might be able to propagate their like? If you did that, you would be consistent, and the native spontaneous expansion which you desire would become possible; but by your hesitation, though you establish indeed village churches, yet you leave those churches unequipped to propagate themselves unless they can obtain the assistance of a bishop who is probably a foreigner.

What answer can I give to that? I am, indeed, sure that to consecrate native village bishops is the true way of expansion. I believe that it would be far safer for the present Bishop of Honan or S. Rhodesia, for instance, to establish a hundred, or two hundred,

---

[1] In the only case in which I have heard of anything like what I have suggested in this chapter being done, I was told that this actually happened.

unpaid native bishops, not assistant bishops, but diocesan bishops ruling over small dioceses consisting of a village or a group of villages, because in ruling such dioceses men would learn the meaning of episcopal authority in its simplest form, and so be prepared to occupy the position of metropolitans as the churches grew in numbers; but if, as Father Kelly said, the idea of a strictly local ministry, unprofessional, untrained and unpaid, seems to be inconceivable, much more does the idea of a local episcopate, unprofessional, untrained and unpaid, seem inconceivable. It is possible that a bishop might be found to ordain local, unpaid, presbyters: that bishops should be found to consecrate local unpaid bishops seems incredible. I may deplore it; but so it is. To ordain only presbyters for the local churches would not be the best, nor the wisest, nor the safest course; but it would be something. It would be a move in the right direction, and it would, I believe, prepare the way for a native episcopate.

VI

The spontaneous expansion of the Church reduced to its elements is a very simple thing. It asks for no elaborate organization, no large finances, no great numbers of paid missionaries. In its beginning it may be the work of one man, and that a man neither learned in the things of this world, nor rich in the wealth of this world. The organization of a little church on the apostolic model is also extremely simple, and the most illiterate converts can use it, and the poorest are sufficiently wealthy to maintain it. Only as it grows and spreads through large provinces and countries do any complex questions arise, and they arise only as a church composed of many little churches is able to produce leaders prepared to handle them by experience learned in the smaller things. There is no need at the beginning to talk of preparing leaders to face great national issues. By the time the issues have become great and complex the leaders of the little churches of today will have learned their lesson, as they cannot possibly be taught it beforehand.

No one, then, who feels within himself the call of Christ to embark on such a path as this need say, I am too ignorant, I am too inexperienced, I have too little influence, or I have not sufficient resources. The first apostles of Christ were in the eyes of the world 'unlearned and ignorant' men: it was not until the Church had endured a persecution and had grown largely in numbers that Christ called a learned man to be His apostle. The missionaries who spread the Gospel and established the Church throughout the lands round the Mediterranean are not known to us as men of great learning or ability. Most of them are not known by name at all. Only when the Church had been established and had spread widely did Christ call the great doctors whose names are familiar to us by their writings, or by their great powers of organization and government.

What is necessary is faith. What is needed is the kind of faith which, uniting a man to Christ, sets him on fire. Such a man can believe that others finding Christ will be set on fire also. Such a man can see that there is no need of money to fill a continent with the knowledge of Christ. Such a man can see that all that is required to consolidate and establish that expansion is the simple application of the simple organization of the Church. It is to men who know that faith, who see that vision, that I appeal. Let them judge what I have written.

II

THE LAW
AND
THE SPIRIT

'St Paul and the Judaizers' is part 2 of a thirty-one page pamphlet published in 1927 under the title *The Establishment of the Church in the Mission Field*. In this selection, Allen deals trenchantly with the issue of 'missionary paternalism.' Selections 6 – 10 are the last five chapters (4 – 8) of the little book entitled *Pentecost and the World* (1917), including a very important footnote to chapter 7. Both 'St Paul and the Judaizers' and *Pentecost and the World* were included in *The Ministry of the Spirit*, the collection of Allen's writings published in 1960, from which the present selections are reproduced.

It will be seen that Allen's doctrine bears upon many proposed innovations for which there is held by some to be no backing in tradition — for example, with respect to the role of women in the Church. It should be noted that Allen wrote out of the Catholic tradition in Anglicanism, not the Evangelical.

5

St Paul and the Judaizers

A. I wonder whether the Bible throws any light on the problem. It might help us to decide what it is wise for us to do. The apostle St Paul, for instance, had to meet this question, and his example and practice might afford some guidance. Have you ever looked at his work from this point of view?

V. Of course I have. I know perfectly well that St Paul established churches just as you seem to want us to do; but it cannot be done today. Some years ago the same man, whose article we were discussing at the beginning, wrote a book on St Paul's missionary method, and plenty of people pointed out at once that the conditions today are utterly different from those which obtained in St Paul's day, and that consequently you cannot argue from his action. I never heard that he made any answer to that.

A. Shall we consider the matter now?

V. If you like.

A. Where shall we begin? Were there any people in the Christian Church in St Paul's day who argued that missions to the heathen ought to be conducted on the same principles which you are maintaining, and for the same reasons?

V. Not that I know of.

A. Were there not people who followed St Paul wherever he went, arguing that Gentile converts must be compelled to keep the law?

V. Oh, you mean the Judaizing party! Of course they did that.

A. Why did they do that?

V. Because they wanted the Jew to be top dog in the church, and the Christian Church to be Jewish throughout, and the converts from the heathen to be admitted only on sufferance, and, in so far as they followed Jewish rules of life, as a species of proselyte.

A. Is that what they said?

V. No, of course they did not put it like that. They said the converts from heathenism could not be saved unless they were circumcised and kept the law. But it amounted to what I said. That would have been the result; and any fool could see it.

A. Do you think those 'certain which came from James' were men who were consciously seeking nothing but to maintain the predominance of the Jews in the church? Do you think that all those who followed them were doing that?

V. I should think they probably were. Anyhow, they were bitter opponents of the policy of St Paul which set the Gentiles free.

A. Was not St Peter at one time inclined to think that they were right?

V. Yes, that is true.

A. And Barnabas also?

V. Yes.

A. And do you think those two men were ready to adopt a policy of which the obvious meaning was nothing but Jewish predominance in the church?

V. No. I should not like to say that. St Peter had gone to the house of Cornelius, and Barnabas had been on a missionary journey with St Paul. I think that they must have had some reason for believing that it was better for the whole body of Christians, Gentiles as well as Jews, that all should be circumcised and keep the law.

A. Do you think that the Galatian and Macedonian converts of St Paul were in danger of being led astray by an appeal which obviously meant nothing but Jewish domination in the church?

V. That seems hardly likely. They must have had some more plausible reason to give.

A. What reason could they have given? What sort of argument could they have used?

V. I do not quite know. All that we are told is that they laid down the law and said that the Gentiles could not be saved unless they kept it.

A. That sounds as if they were, at least professedly, anxious about the salvation of the Gentiles. Perhaps they really were anxious. They might well have been anxious; they might well have believed sincerely that St Paul was leading his converts along a very dangerous path and forsaking the way of Christ in telling them that they need not keep the law. Before the Jerusalem Council they might have sincerely believed that all the apostles would agree with them, and after the Council they might have sincerely believed that they were right. But they must have used some argument to maintain that position. You yourself said that they must have had some reason to give for their belief.

51

V. I am certain that they had some reason.

A. Well, what was it? There are some obvious arguments which they might have used. They might have said, for instance, that Jesus was a Jew and kept the law, and that men who wished to be saved must follow him in this.

V. They might certainly have said that.

A. And did not Jesus say, 'One jot or one tittle shall in no wise pass from the law, till all be fulfilled'? And did not He tell His disciples, 'The Scribes and the Pharisees sit in Moses' seat: all therefore, whatsoever they bid you observe, that observe and do'? Might not these people have argued that Christ the Saviour told His disciples to keep the law?

V. They might. It sounds a strong argument.

A. Might they not then have said that the Jewish law was the Christian law, and must be maintained by Christians?

V. I suppose they might.

A. And might they not have said that if heathen Gentiles were bound by that law the moral standard of the church would be no better than heathen?

V. Well, it is clear from his epistles that even St Paul himself was anxious about the moral standard of the Gentile churches; and that they gave him good cause to be anxious.

A. And might they not have argued that if Gentiles lived in heathen cities and were not bound by the law, the church would certainly be contaminated with heathen ideas of God, and be compromised by compliance with idolatrous customs?

V. I do not know whether they said anything about these things; but I imagine all men would see that strict adherence to the law involved a strict adherence to the idea of God as One and Holy, and would be a great safe-guard against the inroads of heathen conceptions of God, polytheism and idolatry.

A. They might have said so?

V. They certainly might have said so. It would have been a powerful argument.

A. Anyhow, they acted as if they believed it; I suppose I must say that?

V. Yes, you may say that.

A. And is it not more reasonable to suppose that men who plainly had great influence in the church were honest men and used good arguments, even if their hatred and fear of St Paul's doctrine and practice drove them to seek his life, than that they were men who openly and confessedly were fighting for nothing but domination over the Gentile churches? Which do you believe?

V.   I believe that they really were afraid that if St Paul's doctrine of freedom from the law won the day all those evils which you suggested must follow. It seems so perfectly obvious.

A.   Then they shared the fears which you expressed. They in their day and you in yours have felt the same fear, and the same need for a stout maintenance of a standard of morals and doctrine. There is, then, some likeness between the conditions in St Paul's day and in ours.

V.   Well, as far as that goes, there is a resemblance; but I think it ends there. The danger was not so great, because St Paul could always establish his churches with a nucleus of men, Jews and God-fearing Greeks, who really knew the discipline of the law. Now we have nothing of the kind; and that makes so great a difference that it breaks down all argument from St Paul's action.

A.   Let us consider that. What you are saying is that St Paul made converts from the synagogue, Jews and God-fearing Greeks, men who had been trained under the discipline of the law, and therefore he could rely upon them to maintain the Christian standard of doctrine and morals. Is that right?

V.   Yes, that is what I said.

A.   And if we had men like that in the churches today we could follow his example. Is that right?

V.   Yes; no doubt that would be true.

A.   Well, then, let us inquire first whether the converts from the synagogue had such influence in the church that there really was no danger in those days. Did not St Paul write to the Thessalonians as though they had heard of one God living and true from him first?

V.   Yes, that is true.

A.   And does he not write to the Corinthians of the right attitude of Christians to polytheism and to idolatry and idolatrous feasts?

V.   He does.

A.   Why should he do that? If the Pauline churches were really guided by men who had forsaken that sort of error long before he preached to them, if they were not in danger of falling into compromise with heathen ideas of God and heathen immorality, why should he write like that? Was the whole thing a delusion, and was there really no danger at all of the church going astray?

V. No doubt many of the converts were from the heathen outside the synagogue, and they needed this exhortation.

A. But still the nucleus was there, the well-taught, established Jewish converts and proselytes, and there was no fear of the church as a whole going astray. Did not you say that? Didn't you say that St Paul's churches were guided by these men and therefore he could rely upon them to keep the church straight? Was not that the difference between his work and ours which made the imitation of his missionary practice impossible today?

V. Yes, that is true.

A. Then why did they not do their work? Why did they not settle the question? You said that they were the men who saved the church from any danger of compromise with heathen customs and ideas, didn't you? Were these churches really being led by the men upon whom you stake so much? Or were those men comparatively few in number and not always the most influential men in the church?

V. I do not know.

A. But you know, don't you, that very early the breach between the synagogue and the Christian Church became accentuated, so that the Christian could no longer preach in the synagogues. What happened then? Did churches continue to multiply just as before?

V. They certainly multiplied among the Gentiles.

A. In spite of the fact that they could no longer be called 'offshoots of the local synagogue,' as a missionary bishop once called St Paul's churches?

V. Yes, in spite of that.

A. Then may I not conclude that St Paul relied upon neither the Jewish Christians nor Gentile proselytes, but upon something else to maintain and advance the true standard of doctrine and morals in the church? Or must I add further argument?

V. I do not know what further arguments you could adduce.

A. Let us see. I suggested to you a moment ago that the Judaizers must have used some rational argument to bring the Gentiles under the law.

V. Yes. You suggested that they must have taught that the law was the law kept by Christ and confirmed by Him, and that His followers must keep it because He kept it, and apparently told them to keep it.

A. And did you not agree?

V. I agreed that they certainly might have used that argument.

A. And to whom would that argument most strongly appeal: to the Jewish Christians and the God-fearing Greeks who had already accepted the law, or to the Gentile converts who had never been attracted by the law sufficiently strongly to become proselytes?

V. I suppose to the Jewish and God-fearing.

A. Then you think that these classes would be most likely to accept the teaching of the Judaizers?

V. I do.

A. And St Paul was opposed to the Judaizers?

V. Plainly.

A. And he writes as if there were grave danger of his converts submitting to the teaching of the Judaizers?

V. Yes.

A. Then were not those converts from the synagogue rather a source of danger than a source of strength in this controversy? How, then, could St Paul naturally rely upon them? The converted Jews were of the same race as the Judaizers, and had been born under the law; the God-fearing had already submitted. They were the people who would feel least difficulty in acknowledging the truth of the Judaizers' argument.

V. There may be something in that, but still I do not think it very convincing.

A. You mean that you think the Gentile converts would be more ready to accept Jewish claims than the Jewish converts.

V. No; I do not. I do not think either would easily have submitted.

A. Yet you agreed with me that St Paul wrote as if there were grave danger.

V. So I did; but I really do not know what to say about it.

A. Well, let us consider the matter in this way. St Paul relied upon the presence of these converts from the synagogue to maintain the standard of doctrine and morality. You said that, didn't you? Your position was that St Paul's practice was impossible today because we had no such converts upon whom to rely. Is not that what you said?

V. Yes, that is the great difference between his day and ours.

A. May I say, then, that if there had been no converts from the synagogue St Paul would have agreed that the Christian Gentiles must be protected by the hedge of the law?

V.   No, certainly not. St Paul's argument was that men were not to be saved by obedience to law, but by faith in Christ. It does not make the smallest difference to his argument whether there were or were not Jews and God-fearing Greeks in his churches.

A.   Do you mean that he would have spoken and acted exactly as he did, had there been no Jews or God-fearing Greeks in his churches? I thought you said that it was the presence of those men which made all the difference, and that we cannot follow his practice now because there are no Jews or God-fearing Greeks in the churches which we found.

V.   You do not understand. We must have trained men on whom we can rely to maintain some standard. St Paul found those men in the synagogue. That is all that I mean.

A.   And did not find them outside the synagogue?

V.   I should hardly like to say that.

A.   But, surely, you must say that, if you are to maintain your position; because otherwise it is possible that we might find them outside the synagogue today, and that you say we cannot do.

V.   Well, anyhow, we do not. That is the only thing that matters.

A.   Perhaps we do not know, because we have never tried. But did St Paul rely upon the training of the synagogue at all?

V.   Surely he did that. The Jews and God-fearing Greeks brought into the church a well established standard of faith and morals which the Gentile converts sorely lacked. You can hardly deny that.

A.   You mean that these men first learned the discipline of the law, and then, being themselves established in character by that discipline, could accept the liberty of the gospel without danger, and could maintain a standard in the church.

V.   Yes, that is what I mean.

A.   How does that differ from saying that for morality of life Moses with his law is a better and more effective teacher than Christ? Is it not the same as saying that when men have learned the fundamental ideas of morality and of the unity and holiness of God from Moses, then they can accept the faith of Christ without danger; but that the faith of Christ and the teaching of Christ and the grace of Christ and the gift of the Holy Spirit, are not sufficiently powerful by themselves to do what the stern discipline of law alone can do?

V. I cannot say that. I do not believe it. Faith in Christ's grace and His gift of the Holy Spirit are far more strong foundations for purity of life than any law. How can I say that Moses is a better teacher than Christ?

A. But if that is so, it is possible to begin with faith in Christ and to rely solely upon Christ, even if there has been no previous discipline under the law. Does not that follow? And is not that precisely the position which St Paul took up? Did he not teach that for salvation of soul and body in this life and in the life to come, Christ is the only Saviour, and that faith in Him is the only way, and that any trust in the law is vain?

V. That is, I think, what he taught.

A. Then he did not rely upon the discipline of the law, nor did he rely upon the teaching of the synagogue to save the standard of morality in his churches. Whether his converts came from the synagogue or from the heathen world outside, he taught them that they must regard their past ideas as vain, and learn of Christ and of Christ alone, and follow and obey Him, and Him alone? Do you agree?

V. Yes, I agree.

A. May I conclude, then, that this assertion that St Paul's method depended on the presence of proselytes and Jews in his Churches is of no force at all; but is the flat contradiction of his teaching, and would have horrified him?

V. I do not see how it can be avoided. But you must not forget that he preached for the most part to civilized people. Who can tell whether he would have run such risks if he had been face to face with people like those with whom we have to deal in many parts of the world, in Africa, for instance, men with no civilized history behind them, or outcaste tribes in India? There he simply could not have established churches as he did in Galatia or in Macedonia.

A. Why not?

V. Because the people are too degraded.

A. When we hear modern missionaries speaking of their work I do not remember that they ever distinguish in that way. Do they generally say that in dealing with civilized races like the Japanese or the Chinese, they can follow the principles and practice of St Paul because these nations are civilized, but in dealing with outcaste Indians or Africans they cannot follow his example because the people are degraded and uncivilized? Have you ever heard them say anything of that kind?

V.   No, I cannot say that I have.

A.   Would it be possible for them to say it?

V.   No, they could not say it, because we make no such distinction in our action. We follow the same practice everywhere.

A.   But you said that we could not follow the apostolic practice because today the people to whom we go are not as civilized and enlightened as the people to whom St Paul went. Don't you think that the peoples of the Far East would feel insulted if they heard this answer, that they are more degraded that the provincials of Macedonia and of Achaia and of Asia Minor under the Roman Empire? Do you think they would like it?

V.   I never thought of that. I was thinking of uncivilized people in Africa, and I said so.

A.   You did, and I understood you. All that I wanted to do was to suggest that that answer is not a true one. If it were true we should be compelled to make distinctions which we do not make in our mission practice. May I say that whatever the true reason may be, that is not the reason why we do not follow the apostle?

V.   As far as the civilized people are concerned, you may say so; but as for the uncivilized and degraded, it may still be true, that if St Paul had to deal with them he could not have founded churches as he did in the Roman Empire.

A.   Upon what foundation did he build? Did he build on the foundation of the intellectual and social enlightment of the people to whom he went? Did he rely upon that any more than he relied upon the training which the law had given to Jews and proselytes?

V.   No, I do not think that he did that. But still, just think of the conditions in outcaste Indian villages and in African kraals!

A.   I am thinking of them. I am prepared to admit anything, however bad, that may be said of them. But I am thinking of St Paul's principles: circumstances do not alter principles. And was not his principle that Christ sufficed to meet all conditions?

V.   No doubt; but there is a limit beyond which no man can go. Surely you recognize a *praeparatio evangelica*: the people to whom St Paul went were prepared by a long discipline under law, so that their moral and religious sense was cultivated. What Africa needs is a like preparation. I have heard missionaries say that what Africans need is a long discipline under the terrors of the moral law, then they might be prepared to receive the Gospel; but as it is they have had no moral training to keep them straight. To talk about Pauline principles in such a case is mere folly.

A. I, too, have heard them say that; but is it true? I have heard others speak very differently; but I do not want to weigh authority against authority on this subject. That would be an endless and futile task. What you and I want to consider is, what is the truth of the gospel. And we agreed, did we not, that Christ is a better foundation on which to build than Moses?

V. Yes, we did.

A. And shall we not agree that when missionaries of the gospel go to any people, it is because in the providence of God the time has come for them to go?

V. That is certain.

A. And can missionaries of the gospel be missionaries of anything but the gospel?

V. Certainly not.

A. Then in the providence of God the time has come for these people to hear the gospel.

V. Plainly.

A. Then it is of Christ that they must hear, not of the law; for the law is not the gospel.

V. Well.

A. And moral advance must spring from faith in Christ and obedience to Him, not from fear of the law.

V. Well.

A. You say, 'Well,' but what do you really mean; do you mean that in the case of these degraded people the indwelling Christ is to be put first as the foundation of all, and not some external control?

V. I really do not know what to say. It seems a fearful risk.

A. Do you agree with me that St Paul's principle that the indwelling Christ is the one and only hope for men would have forced him to act in Africa today as he did in Macedonia and in Galatia twenty centuries ago, or do you think that he would have said that he could apply that doctrine in Galatia and Macedonia, but that in Africa external control was unavoidable? Is his doctrine one which could so change?

V. Well, he might have done it; but we cannot venture so far.

A. Why not, if indeed we believe in Christ?

V. It is all very well to believe in Christ; we all do that; but to say that Africans can do without control from us, that is going too far. Didn't I tell you long ago that we are sent to control, and must control?

A. Now you are explaining why our practice is identical in principle in the Far East and in Africa; for if we believe that we must rely upon our control to save our converts, and if we teach our converts to rely upon our control, that can be applied universally. They are all new-born Christians, and we can easily be afraid for them all, and see at once that they all alike need our control.

V. That is right. You see that at last.

A. Do you remember that, when I asked you why the Judaizers acted as they did, you answered that they obviously wanted the Jew to be top dog in the church, and converts from the heathen to be admitted only so far as they followed Jewish rules of life. You are not afraid that our converts may one day say that of us?

V. Some of them say it now; they accuse us of importing western forms and civilization, and of keeping them down, but it is absurdly false. We do nothing of the kind. Our one care is for their progress and stability.

A. Did not the Judaizers say that, or might they not have said that, and yet you, looking at their work from this distance, said at once that it was plain that they were working to maintain the supremacy of the Jews in the church, and to keep all Gentile converts in the position of proselytes? Have those natives who accuse us of keeping them down no reason or excuse?

V. No excuse whatever. It is perfectly manifest to any impartial observer that we use our control solely for their uplift, and have no idea whatever of maintaining our supremacy, or of keeping them down. It is absurd and wicked to suggest such a notion.

A. Yet our converts say it. It is strange.

6

The Spirit Revealing the Need of Men

We have seen that the apostles, inspired by the Holy Ghost, began to preach Christ as the Saviour. Under the influence of the Holy Spirit, not only were their minds illuminated to see that the name of Jesus could be glorified and His claims vindicated in no other way than by the salvation of men in Him; they themselves were filled with a desire for the salvation of men akin to that desire which led Him to take upon Him human flesh.

But there was not only a great desire to glorify Christ by the salvation of men in Him; there was also a profound conviction that men needed Christ. The apostles were persuaded that the preaching of the gospel was of such vital importance to men that no pains or penalties could be allowed to postpone it. With the consciousness of power to give they attained consciousness also of the deep need of human souls.

This consciousness is shown not only by the fact of their preaching, but by the character of their preaching. It might indeed be possible to read the speech of St Stephen in the Council (7.) and to suppose that this preaching was simply the expression of a great loyalty to the Person of Jesus, such loyalty as we have often read of in history. His Master had been wickedly misjudged, wrongfully condemned, and ignominiously executed. He was full of righteous indignation. He was determined to defend His Master at all costs. He was determined to set the baseness of his opponents in the strongest light. He therefore searches the history of his nation for examples of the betrayal and rejection of God's servants to find a parallel for the iniquity of his opponents, and proclaims that He whom they cast out is now at the right hand of God. There is a certain fury in his speech which might justify such an interpretation. But the general course of the history recounted in Acts forbids us to think that St Luke intended to represent the apostles as moved by such motives. The preaching is begun in Jerusalem, but it is carried into wider and wider fields to men who had very little immediate connexion with the surrender of Jesus to Pilate. The preaching to them is not merely an appeal from the prejudiced to the unprejudiced in order to win a general recognition of the truth and goodness of a martyr. It is certainly inspired by a desire to win men to believe in Jesus as the Messiah, the Saviour; but it is equally certainly inspired by a conviction that the men to whom the preaching is delivered need Christ.

This becomes still more plain when we consider the conclusion to which the preaching always leads. St Peter, preaching to the people in Jerusalem (2), justifies Jesus; but his object is not merely the justification of Jesus. When the consciences of his hearers are touched and they ask, 'What shall we do?' he is not satisfied. His desire for the recognition of the grace and glory of Jesus takes a new form—desire for the salvation of his hearers. 'Repent,' he says, 'and be baptized every one of you in the name of Jesus Christ, unto the remission of sins, and ye shall receive the gift of the Holy Ghost' (2.38). Again in the Temple it is for the 'blotting out of their sins' that he urges them to repent (3.19). Even in the Council itself he is not content to argue from the healing of the lame man a justification of Jesus: it is 'salvation in his name,' which he proclaims (4.12). Again, in the Council he gives as his reason why he and his fellow apostles must continue to preach the truth that God exalted Jesus 'to be a prince and a saviour for to give repentance to Israel and forgiveness of sins' (5. 31). And so to Cornelius the end of his teaching is remission of sins (10.43).

In the account of St Paul's work, the need of men for Christ takes a most prominent place. Forgiveness of sins (13.38), 'eternal life' (13.46, 48), 'the way of salvation' (16.17, 31), take as important a place in his preaching as 'that Jesus is the Christ' (17.3; 18.5). Indeed, before Agrippa he sums up his work rather in terms of the need of men than in terms of the demonstration of the glory of Jesus. He says that his commission from the Lord was 'to open their eyes that they may turn from darkness to light and from the power of Satan unto God, that they may receive remission of sins and an inheritance among them that are sanctified by faith in me' (26.18).

The apostles preached as men who were convinced that men needed repentance and remission of sins. They preached repentance; they preached remission of sins in the name of Jesus; they preached a baptism in the name of Jesus Christ for the remission of sins.

The apostles had, in the early days of their discipleship, preached repentance and baptism; they had been familiar with the preaching of John the Baptist; but the repentance and baptism which they now preached were very different from the repentance and baptism which they had preached before Pentecost. Before Pentecost they had preached as the Baptist had preached. The Baptist had preached that men should turn from their sins, from those offences against the moral law of which they knew that they had been guilty; his baptism was a washing from these. Such repentance, such baptism, was essentially limited in its scope: it dealt only with sins known to the penitent; it referred primarily to the abandonment of evil courses; it left the penitent in the same spiritual state in which he began; it brought him no new power nor any new source of life. But now the apostles preached a repentance which was rather positive than negative. They preached not simply that men should turn from sin, but that they should turn to Christ. Repentance for sin which did not bring men to Christ was no longer adequate; for to turn to Christ is a far larger and more vital act than mere turning from known sin. To turn from known sin by turning to Christ is to do more than to turn from known sin; it is to turn from all sin known and unknown. What men turn to is more important than what they turn from, even if that to which they turn is only a higher moral truth; but to turn to Christ is far more than to turn to higher moral truth: it is to turn the face towards Him in whom is all moral truth; it is to turn to Him in whom is not only the virtue which corresponds to the known vice from which the penitent desires to flee, but all virtue; it is to turn the face to all holiness, all purity, all grace. It was this repentance which the apostles preached after Pentecost.

And the baptism corresponded to the repentance. Baptism was no longer the mere symbolical washing away of known sin; it was baptism into Jesus Christ. It was translation into a new spiritual state. It brought the promise of the gift of the Holy Spirit. It brought new life, new power. It brought men into touch with Jesus Christ, the source of all truth and grace. It opened to them the inexhaustible treasures of the life of Christ. It bound them to Him. However little they might understand at the moment of their baptism, by that baptism they did actually enter upon that new life of union with Christ, of obedience to Christ, of grace derived from Christ, which must inevitably draw them from all sin into the holiness and love of

Christ. Baptism into Christ implied a new conception of salvation, a new way of salvation, a way which was to be found only in Christ.

Because repentance, which is a turning to Christ, is a turning from and a forsaking of all sin, because baptism into Christ is not only a washing from known sin but the creation of a new relationship to Christ, because that union brings with it the promised gift of the Holy Spirit, the source of all holiness, the assurance of perfect holiness, because all salvation is in Christ and in the reception of His Spirit, the repentance and baptism which the apostles preached was 'unto remission of sins.' There was a real release.

That was why people who had repented, people who had been baptized with John's baptism, must repent again in a very different way, and be baptized with a baptism which could never be repeated. That was what men needed, not simply sorrow for past sin and a putting away of their wrong-doing and a resolve to amend, but a coming to Christ, an acceptance of Christ, the gift of the Holy Spirit. Men needed this repentance, this baptism unto remission of sins, this gift of the Holy Spirit. In the very beginning of the Acts the baptism of John is contrasted with baptism with the Holy Spirit. In the very first sermon of St Peter the Holy Spirit is promised to those who were baptized in the name of Jesus Christ unto the remission of sins (2.38). This note rings through the Acts. St Paul at Ephesus found certain disciples, and asked, 'Into what were ye baptized?' And they said, 'Into John's baptism.' Then said Paul: 'John verily baptized with the baptism of repentance, saying unto the people that they should believe on him which should come after him, that is, on Jesus. When they heard this they were baptized in the name of the Lord Jesus. And when Paul had laid his hands upon them the Holy Ghost came upon them' (19.2-6). Here clearly John's baptism is contrasted with baptism in the name of Jesus unto remission of sins and the gift of the Holy Ghost. Repentance was good, but it was not sufficient. Men needed remission of sins and the Holy Ghost.

The Apostles preached as men who were convinced that the need of men could only be satisfied by the gift of the Holy Spirit. It is here, in the close connexion between the preaching of the remission of sins and the gift of the Holy Spirit, that St Luke reveals most clearly his understanding of that hemisphere of the Holy Spirit which St Paul's epistles more clearly state. The hemisphere of redeeming love is in the Acts more definitely revealed; but the hemisphere of sanctification is not unrevealed. Remission of sins was preached in the name of Jesus; in the name of Jesus converts were baptized; in the name of Jesus the Holy Ghost was given. In Jesus was remission of sins, in Jesus forgiveness, in Jesus justification, in Jesus partaking of the Holy Ghost, whose presence in the soul makes remission and forgiveness and sanctification possible.

They preached as men who were convinced that the need of men could be satisfied only in Jesus Christ. 'There is none other name under heaven given among men,' said St Peter (4.12), and St Paul's preaching was that 'by him every one that believeth is justified from all things, from which ye could not be justified by the law of Moses.' (13.39). There is in the preaching in the Acts a grave and solemn note. To reject Jesus is to forfeit the remission of sins. 'Save yourselves,' says St Peter, 'from this untoward generation' (2.40). 'Beware,' cries St Paul, 'lest that come upon you which is spoken in the prophets; Behold, ye despisers, and wonder and perish' (13.39, 40). It is possible for them 'to judge themselves unworthy of eternal life' (13.46). When they persistently opposed themselves he uttered the solemn warning, 'Your blood be upon your own heads' (18.6). St Paul did not hesitate to speak of 'the wrath to come' (I Thess. 1.10). The very notion of salvation on which the apostles laid so much stress implied a danger and a serious danger, a need and an urgent need. They preached Christ as the Saviour and as the only Saviour, 'knowing the terror of the Lord' (II Cor. 5.11).

This is also the attitude of the gospels. In them too the love of the Father who sent the Son, and the love of the Son who came, is associated with the forgiveness of sins, with a deep need of men which nothing but the Passion of the Son of God could supply. The love of God was so great, the need of men was so great, that nothing short of the Incarnation and the Passion could satisfy it. The realization of the one and the realization of the other are closely united. And as in the gospels it was the love of God which first discerned the need, not the recognition of his need by man which first made him send up a great cry to God for help; so in the Acts it was the coming of the Spirit of Christ into the souls of men which led them to see the need of their fellow-men. It was the Holy Spirit who taught St Paul to know 'darkness' and 'the power of Satan.'

The apostles were profoundly conscious of the need of men for Christ, yet there are sayings in Acts, as in the gospels, which seem to make that need appear less. In the gospels, for instance, there is a description of the judgment of the nations (St Matt. 25.31-46). There, men are represented as accepted by Christ on the ground that they have done well, that their actions partook of His nature of charity. So in the Acts, St Peter declares to Cornelius that 'in every nation he that feareth God and worketh righteousness is accepted with him' (10.35). And St Paul, who says that he preaches to those 'who are perishing' (I Cor. 1.18), says also that God 'will render to every man according to his works: to them who by patient continuance in well-doing seek for glory and honour and immortality, eternal life . . . glory and honour and peace to every man that worketh good, to the Jew first, and also to the Greek' (Rom. 2.6-10).

Now there is certainly a difficulty in reconciling the apostolic insistence upon the need of men, the apostolic assertion that men are in darkness, under the power of Satan and can be saved only in Christ, with this more comfortable doctrine that everybody, everywhere, whatever their religious beliefs, whatever their ignorance of Christ, will yet be accepted with God, if they obey the law written in their hearts.

We are familiar with these two apparently opposite doctrines in their modern form, each overstated and brought into the most extreme opposition, and in this modern form we reject them both. We have heard men talk of so many millions of souls passing into a Christless eternity within the space of time occupied by their speeches. That has struck us as horrible. We have heard men argue that it is most intolerant to imagine that the heathen so need Christ that they cannot be saved without Him, that it is a libel on the fatherhood of God to speak of men as 'perishing in their ignorance.' That strikes us as extraordinarily flabby. It is certainly not conformable to our strongest convictions about the Incarnation.

Still, the opposition is perplexing. We can understand how the conviction that all men need Christ with the deepest and most strong need can make men zealous missionaries. But this world-wide optimism, this conviction that heathen who serve God as they have been taught, and work righteousness as they can, are accepted with God, seems to weaken the missionary claim. We can hardly expect people to be as fervent in the propagation of the gospel if the heathen know enough to be saved, and if it will be well with them if only they do what they now know to be right. And we see that, in fact, many use this argument to justify lukewarmness in the support of, or even active opposition to, missions to the heathen. We feel almost compelled to accept one alternative or the other, either the apostolic doctrine of need so urgent, so instant, that nothing can be allowed to delay, or to prevent, the propagation of the gospel at all costs, or the equally apostolic doctrine of 'glory, honour, and peace to every man that worketh good,' and then the need for the propagation of the gospel seems to be less urgent.

In face of this difficulty it is well to return to the Acts and to read again the history recorded by St Luke. The apostolic missionaries, in his story, saw both sides of this question, they stated both sides, yet their zeal was not diminished at all. On the contrary, they lived and died in earnest, eager effort to bring the world to Christ. That is the fact set before us in the Acts. Obviously hope for the heathen does not necessarily weaken zeal for the propagation of the gospel.

The solution of the difficulty does not lie in the intellectual, but in the spiritual sphere. It is to be found in experience of the Holy Spirit, in an experience of His influence like theirs. It was the Holy Spirit who came to them with the fire of divine love. It was His presence which made them missionaries. Missionary zeal does not grow out of intellectual beliefs, nor out of theological arguments, but out of love. If I do not love a person I am not moved to help him by proofs that he is in need; if I do love him I wait for no proof of special need to urge me to help him. Knowledge of Christ is so rich a treasure that the spirit of love must necessarily desire to impart it. The mere assurance that others have it not is sufficient proof of their need. This spirit of love throws aside intellectual arguments that they can do very well without it. But if this spirit is not present, a man is easily persuaded that to impart a knowledge of Christianity (for it is noteworthy that such men always speak of Christianity rather than of Christ) is not necessary, nay, is superfluous expense of energy which might be better used in other ways.

The Holy Spirit is revealed in the Acts as the teacher of the need of men for Christ, because He illuminates men so that they see Christ, and know Christ for themselves. For themselves knowledge of Christ is an unspeakable necessity. When once the Holy Spirit reveals Christ to the soul, whatever the previous religion or morality of the man may have been, he is conscious that he could not do without Christ. Rob him of Christ, and he is robbed of all. It is wholly inconceivable that he should look back with satisfaction upon himself as he was without Christ. It is wholly inconceivable that he should think of himself as being saved without Christ then, and being saved in Christ now. 'Perishing in his ignorance' is not too strong a description for him. He knows that is exactly what he was. Then if he looks out into the world he sees men who do not know Christ. Their religion may be better or worse than his own early religion was; but he sees that in heathen lands men are living in sin, in sin which they know to be sin, in a social order where sin is an all-pervading force. He sees that they do not know Christ. He knows what his own state was before Jesus Christ was revealed to him. He knows that they have not that revelation of Jesus Christ. What can he say? 'Perishing in their ignorance' is not too strong an expression.

Yet, knowing the hopelessness of his own case without Christ, knowing the hopelessness of their case without Christ, there is, nevertheless, a hope. The Spirit of Christ is a Spirit quick to recognize and welcome signs of goodness, even as the spirit of love in human hearts is quick to welcome and recognize the least sign of goodness in those whom they deeply love. 'A cup of cold water' appears to the Spirit of love a sign of kinship with Christ; alms and prayers appear to that Spirit proofs of capacity to receive Christ; any striving after truth, any seeking after God if haply they may feel after Him and find Him will open at once the door of hope. Here is the sign. Here is a soul not remote from Christ. The Spirit of Christ goes out to him, with love, and approval, and thankfulness. It welcomes him. God accepts him. 'In every nation he that feareth God and worketh righteousness is accepted with him.' The Spirit of Christ knows it and rejoices in it.

This is no intellectual solution of the apparent opposition. If we treat the question as one to be viewed from the outside, impersonally; if we are content to weigh the one argument against the other; above all, if we welcome the sense of freedom from responsibility which a benevolent optimism might seem to induce, there is little doubt that we shall explain away the sterner teaching of the apostles, and welcome their expressions of universal hope as the larger truth. But then, since that attitude relieves us of all sense of need for active propagation of the gospel, it undermines all true understanding of the activity and zeal of the apostles. Their fervour must seem to us rather exaggerated, and we cannot possibly understand the Acts of the Apostles.

Nay, more, if we allow the consideration of heathen morality and heathen religion to absolve us from the duty of preaching the gospel we are really deposing Christ from His throne in our own souls. If we admit that men can do very well without Christ, we accept the Saviour only as a luxury for ourselves. If they can do very well without Christ, then so could we. This is to turn our backs upon the Christ of the gospels and the Christ of Acts and to turn our faces towards law, morality, philosophy, natural religion.

We look at the moral teaching of some of the heathen nations and we find it higher than we had expected to find it. We ask, 'What more do they need? They know what is right. They know enough. They know more than they can practise. To teach them more would only be to set them a standard still further above them.' Or we look at morality in Christian lands, and we begin to wonder whether our practice is really much higher than theirs, and we say, 'They are very well as they are. Leave them alone.'

When we so speak and think we are treating the question of the salvation of men exactly as we should have treated it had Christ never appeared in the world at all. It is an essentially pre-Christian attitude, and implies that the Son of God has not been delivered for our salvation. It suggests that the one and only way of salvation known to me is to keep the commandments. That was indeed true before the coming of the Son of God, before the Passion, before the Resurrection, before Pentecost; but after Pentecost that is no longer true. After Pentecost the answer to any man who inquires the way of salvation is no longer 'Keep the law,' but, 'Believe in the Lord Jesus Christ.' The one question of vital importance is not, 'Do you keep the law?' but, 'Did you receive the Holy Ghost when you believed?'

Similarly, we look at the religious systems of the East, and we find in them much truth. We say, 'How beautiful! How good! What sublime thoughts about the Deity are expressed here! Why should we disturb the confidence of the people in such a belief as this?' The answer is equally clear in the gospels and in Acts. No belief which men had ever held was superior to Judaism, if there was any to equal it; no philosophy was better than that of the best Greek teachers. Had they sufficed, there had been no Passion of the Son of God. The apostles, inspired by the Holy Ghost, were troubled with no doubts whether the monotheism of the Jews or the philosophy of the Greeks were sufficient for their salvation. Filled with the Spirit, they were certain that both Jews and Greeks needed Christ, and that neither Jewish monotheism nor Greek philosophy would do instead.

When, then, we speak as though heathen moral teaching and heathen philosophical speculation absolved us from the duty of preaching Christ, if this is anything more than an excuse of idleness, if it really represents our religious belief, then it is a turning back from Christ to another gospel, which is not another, to a way of salvation well known before Christ came. When once men have done that in their own souls, it is not surprising that what they choose for themselves they find sufficient for others. We ought not to preach Christ, men say, because the morals and philosophy of the people are good! How does that absolve us? To those who so speak Christianity is a system of morals and philosophy, perhaps a little better than others, but essentially of the same order, better suited to us perhaps from any other system, but not essential, and therefore not of sufficient importance to justify us in disturbing ancestral beliefs.

Such conceptions of Christianity have nothing in common with the conceptions which lie at the back of the book of Acts or with the spirit of its author. They are the flat contradiction of the whole teaching of the Acts, and the denial of the Spirit there revealed as the 'Spirit of Christ and of God.' If they had been prevalent in the Church in the days which immediately followed Pentecost the history of the Church would have been a very different one. To read Acts with understanding, we must know, with the real knowledge born of experience, that the Spirit of Christ, the Spirit of the Incarnation and the Passion, the Spirit given at Pentecost, is the answer of God to a real need of the world, that is of every single soul in the world; for in the Acts these two meet, the redeeming Spirit and the utter need, and it is the redeeming Spirit that reveals the utter need.

7

The Administration of the Spirit

The apostles, moved by the Spirit, went forth as ministers of the Spirit. As ministers of the Spirit, they did not simply preach Jesus and the Resurrection, and so lead men to repentance and to faith in Christ; they communicated to others the Spirit which they themselves had received. They not only revealed the Spirit by their words and deeds, they not only convinced men that they had received the Spirit, but they administered the Spirit.

There are in the Acts a few accounts of the setting apart of Christians for special work in the Church by the laying on of hands. The seven were so ordained in Jerusalem by the apostles (6.6); Paul and Barnabas were so set apart in Antioch for their missionary work (13.3); and it is almost universally agreed, though it is not definitely stated by St Luke, that the elders were so ordained in the churches of Galatia (14.23).

In these accounts it is interesting to note:

First, that in none of these cases does St Luke assert that there was any gift of the Holy Spirit then given. Such a gift, a special gift for special work, there probably was. Such a gift is certainly suggested by St Paul's words to the Ephesian elders when he reminded them that the Holy Ghost had made them overseers (20.28); such a gift is certainly suggested by St Paul's charge to Timothy: 'Stir up the gift that is in thee through the laying on of my hands' (II Tim. 1.6), 'and of the presbytery' (I Tim. 4.14); but, if there was a gift, St Luke does not call attention to it.

Secondly, it is noticeable that St Luke constantly tells us that the persons upon whom hands were laid for some special office in the Church were men who had already received the Holy Spirit. This is definitely stated in the case of the seven (6.3) and of St Paul (9.17) and of Barnabas (11.24). Similarly, we are told of the disciples at Antioch in Pisidia that they were 'filled with joy and with the Holy Spirit' (13.52) before their elders were appointed (14.23). Indeed it is apparent that men were everywhere chosen for special office in the Church because they were full of the Holy Spirit.

These two considerations, that St Luke does not mention any gift of the Holy Spirit at the time of ordination, whilst he does notice the fact that the men so set apart were men already full of the Holy Spirit, must be enough to satisfy us that is was not in these cases that St Luke perceived the peculiar glory of that administration of the Spirit which began at Pentecost. Every reader of the Old Testament was familiar with passages which spoke of the imparting of a Spirit to men appointed to special work, by the laying on of the hands of inspired men, or by an anointing. The idea was quite familiar. What was not familiar, what was indeed peculiar to the new dispensation, was the communication of the Spirit to the whole body of Christians, and to every individual member of the body. That those who were possessed with the Spirit should lay hands on common men that they might be filled with the Spirit for their common daily life as Christians, was marvellously strange. It exalted the common life of common men to heights before held only by some special and important service of God. It exalted men occupied in humble tasks of daily toil to the position before peculiar to prophets and kings and priests. Christians all became kings and priests (Rev. 1.6; I Pet. 2.9); the Church became a kingdom of priests.

This laying of hands upon all who were baptized that they might receive the Holy Spirit seems to have been the universal practice. It is true that St Luke does not repeat again and again in every place that the apostles laid their hands on their converts that they might receive the Holy Spirit. But he begins with a promise made to the multitude by St Peter that if they would repent and believe in Jesus, they should receive the gift of the Holy Spirit (2.38); and he goes on to declare that St Peter asserted to the Council that this promise had actually been fulfilled (5.32). He then particularly explains what happened in Samaria: 'Now when the apostles which were at Jerusalem heard that Samaria had received the word of God, they sent unto them Peter and John, who when they were come down prayed for them, that they might receive the Holy Ghost; for as yet he was fallen upon none of them, only they were baptized in the name of the Lord Jesus. Then laid they their hands on them, and they received the Holy Ghost' (8.14-17). He further tells us what happened when St Paul met at Ephesus disciples who had been baptized into John's baptism, how he directed them to be baptized in the name of the Lord Jesus, and laid his hands upon them and the Holy

Ghost came on them (19.5, 6). Though he does not repeat again the like event in the case of each convert, he implies that they all everywhere did receive the gift, as when he says of the disciples at Antioch in Pisidia that they were filled with joy and with the Holy Ghost (13.52), though he has not mentioned any laying on of hands. This is borne out by the epistles of St Paul, who writes to his converts in Galatia, or in Thessalonica, or in Corinth as to men perfectly familiar with the gift of the Holy Spirit.

That St Luke considered the gift of the Holy Spirit necessary for every Christian is certain; consequently it seems strange that, in his account of the missionary preaching of St Paul, he never once mentions the promise of the Holy Spirit nor any teaching concerning that gift. I have before pointed out that the sermons and speeches of St Paul, as recorded in Acts, do not contain any complete statement of St Paul's gospel, and that a fuller statement can be gathered from the I Thessalonians alone than from any speech or sermon in Acts.[1] The fact that in these speeches and sermons there is no teaching about the Holy Spirit, a teaching which St Paul certainly gave to his converts, and which he certainly considered vital, makes this conclusion the more secure. St Luke, in reporting St Paul's speeches to particular people in particular places, was not setting forth his gospel in any fullness, but was accurately reporting what St Paul actually said under the special circumstances to the particular audience before him.

St Luke certainly teaches that the Holy Spirit was given to all the members of the Christian body; his language would certainly lead us to believe that the gift was administered by the laying on of hands of the apostles; nevertheless, it is remarkable that of the four cases in which he actually gives us any details there should be two in which the laying on of hands by one of the Twelve is definitely excluded. In the first of these St Luke tells us that St Paul, after his wonderful conversion, received the gift of the Holy Spirit by the laying on of hands (9.17); but he also expressly states the name of the minister, and the minister is not one of the inner circle of apostles. In the second case he expressly states that the gift was given without any human intermediary at all (10.44; 11.15; 15.8).

It is indeed strange that St Luke should have given us such very different accounts of the manner in which the gift was given; once by

[1] *Missionary Methods: St Paul's or Ours?*, chapter 7.

the laying on of the hands of St Peter and St John, once by the laying on of the hands of Ananias, once by the laying on of the hands of St Paul, and once in the presence of St Peter without any laying on of hands. When we consider how frequently reference is made in this book to the Holy Spirit, and how important St Luke manifestly considered the gift to be, it is indeed hard to escape from the conclusion that he was far more profoundly concerned with the reality and universality of the gift than he was with the mode of the administration of the gift. That which was of primary importance in his eyes was the presence of the Spirit, the gift of the Spirit, the certainty of the presence, the certainty of the gift; the means by which the gift was received seems to have been stated rather to assure us of the certainty of the fact than for its own importance.

In saying this I do not deny that there was a normal manner and means by which the gift was administered. That means doubtless was the laying on of apostolic hands. I do not wish to deny that St Luke teaches us a very important fact when he assures us that the gift was administered by the laying on of the apostles' hands. But I think it is useful to observe how the emphasis is laid by St Luke; for I perceive that we are often in danger of laying the greater emphasis on that upon which he laid the less. Some of our teachers speak of the allusions in the Acts as though the laying on of apostolic hands was the one point of vital importance, whereas St Luke writes as though the gift of the Holy Spirit were the one thing of vital importance, by whatever means that gift was conveyed, whether with, or without, the external act.

The apostles, then, did manifestly go forth as men moved by the Spirit to communicate the Spirit to others. The Holy Ghost was promised, the Holy Ghost was ministered. 'If the ministration of death written and engraven in stones was glorious, so that the children of Israel could not steadfastly behold the face of Moses for the glory of his countenance; which glory was to be done away: how shall not the ministration of the Spirit be rather glorious?' (II Cor. 3.7, 8). Glorious it was, glorious it remains.

This administration of the Spirit is the key of the apostolic work. It alone explains the promise of remission of sins in the preaching of the apostles. It alone explains the assurance of forgiveness which filled the hearts of their converts. It alone explains the new power which was manifested in the life of the Christian Church, the new striving after holiness, the new charity expressed in organized form for the amelioration of the sufferings of the poorer brethren. It alone explains the certainty of the hope of eternal life which filled the souls of the Christians and enabled them to face persecution and martyrdom. It alone explains the new sense of the value and dignity of the body which led to a new enthusiasm for purity of life and created hospitals for the care of the diseased. It alone explains the zeal for the salvation of men, which carried the gospel of Christ throughout the then known world.

8

The Spirit the Source and Test of New Forms of Missionary Activity

In the Acts there is revealed a most curious change in the conduct of the apostles before and after Pentecost. Whether St Luke deliberately desired to call our attention to this change is not clear; but in his narrative the change is very apparent. Before Pentecost the apostles are represented as acting under the influence of an intellectual theory; after Pentecost they are represented as acting under the impulse of the Spirit.

The only event recorded after the Ascension before Pentecost is the appointment of Matthias. This appointment was made, we are told, at the instigation of St Peter, and the speech in which he urged it upon his fellow apostles is reported. St Peter found a passage in the Old Testament which seemed to him to foretell the defection of Judas. This passage ended with the words, 'His office let another take.' From this St Peter concluded that the apostles ought to choose a man to fill the position left vacant by the death of the traitor. Here there is implied an argument which is yet more clearly expressed in the prayer which follows: 'Thou Lord, which knowest the hearts of all men, show of these two the one whom thou hast chosen, to take the place in this ministry and apostleship, from which Judas fell away.' The argument is that Christ appointed twelve apostles: that one had fallen away and perished: the number of the apostles was therefore incomplete: consequently it was the duty of the apostles to restore it by appointing a new member.

Convinced by this argument, they resolved to appoint one of those who had been with them from the beginning and was a witness of the Resurrection. There were many who satisfied these conditions. In order to determine which of these should be appointed to the vacant office, they first selected two, and then adopted a method commonly practised in the Old Testament to discover the will of God: they cast lots. The lot fell upon Matthias, and he was numbered with the eleven apostles.

By casting lots the apostles revealed that they had not that clear and intuitive apprehension of the will of God which sometimes marked the actions of some of the Old Testament prophets. When Samuel, for instance, went to Bethlehem, and Jesse made his sons to pass before him, the prophet, as he viewed each one, was perfectly clear that he knew the mind of God. 'The Lord hath not chosen this,' he said again and gain, until it almost appeared that he had rejected the whole family. At last, when David was sent for and brought in, he recognized at once the man whom the Lord had chosen, and anointed him. The apostles had not this certain knowledge: they adopted a method used by those who were in doubt as to the mind of God.

Thus, in the account given by St Luke of the appointment of Matthias, these two points stand out with remarkable clearness: first, that the action of the apostles was based upon an intellectual theory, and secondly that they had no definite spiritual guidance which revealed to them unmistakably any individual disciple as called by Christ to the apostolate.

After Pentecost a very remarkable change is to be seen. The apostles no longer argue: they obey a spiritual impulse. They do not act in obedience to the dictates of an intellectual theory; the one and only guide, both in their own actions and in their judgment of the action of others, is their recognition of the Spirit in themselves and others.

I have already pointed out that St Peter expressed a great understanding of the nature and work of Jesus in his first sermon; but neither he nor his fellow apostles had intellectually grasped the truth which he expressed. They did not begin their work with a reasoned theory. They did not argue that, the nature and work of Christ being universal, they must embrace the whole world in their view. Christ taught this; but the apostles did not grasp it at once. Their view was limited, their understanding partial. But neither did they begin with a theory of the nature and work of Christ, or of the character of their mission which excluded the greater part of the human race, a theory which needed to be revised and corrected as time went on and larger and truer conceptions were admitted. Their view was partial, but it was not false; it was limited, but it was not misleading. So far as they could see, they spoke truly of Christ and of their work; nay, more, they spoke in terms which embraced more than they understood.

This was due to the fact that they did not begin their work under the direction of an intellectual theory, but under the impulse of the Spirit. This Spirit was in its nature world-wide, all-embracing. Consequently they did not gradually enlarge their sympathies, and extend their activities in obedience to the demands of an intellectual progress; the world-embracing spirit enlarged and expanded their sympathy, and intellectual illumination followed. They then perceived the wider and larger application of truths of which they had hitherto seen only the partial application. Study of the doctrine did not lead to the wider activity; enlarged activity led them to understand the doctrine.

Similarly, their sense of the need of men for Jesus Christ was essentially the apprehension of a universal truth. Wherever they might meet men, the men whom they met would share that need which they knew first for themselves and for their fellow countrymen. If they knew the need at all, they knew it for the world. Consequently, when they expressed it, though their thoughts at the moment were turned to a special limited class of men, yet the expression took universal form. They did not argue that the need of this class of men, or of that race of men, was great, and that therefore they must take steps to supply the need. They were moved, not so much by an intellectual apprehension, as by a spiritual illumination. They met men, and the need of those men whom they met cried aloud to them. Their own desire for the revelation of the glory of Jesus in the salvation of men went out towards those whom they met, and was immediately answered by the recognition of the need of those whom they met for Jesus Christ.

Again, Christ had given them a world-wide commission, embracing all the nations; but intellectually they did not understand what He meant. They found that out as they followed the impulse of the Spirit.

They did not base their action upon any intellectual interpretation of the nature and work and command of Christ. Neither did they base their action upon any anticipation of results which might be expected to follow from it. They did not argue that the conversion of any particular class or race of men might be expected greatly to strengthen the Church for her work in the world and therefore they ought to make special efforts to win the adhesion of this class or race. They did not argue that the relaxation or abandonment of familiar rules would inevitably result in serious injury to the Church. They

did argue that any particular action of a missionary was to be condemned because, if it were approved, it would seem to undermine
some generally accepted doctrine, or would greatly disturb the minds
of a large body of Christians, or would lead to developments which
might be undesirable. The apostles acted under the impulse of the
Spirit; their action was not controlled by the exigencies of any
intellectual theory.

This is most manifest in those steps towards the evangelization of
the Gentiles upon which St Luke lays special stress. Philip the Evangelist went to meet the Ethiopian under the direct influence of the
Spirit, and baptized him without apparently drawing, or expecting
others to draw, any conclusions from his action which might involve
the whole Church in a policy. In the crucial case of the visit of St
Peter to Cornelius, St Peter himself was prepared by a special vision,
and evidently realized that his action was liable to be called in question; but he acted under the impulse of the Spirit, though neither he
nor the others really understood what consequences were involved in
his action. St Peter certainly did not think the matter out, decide
that the Gentiles were within the terms of Christ's commission, and
then, and therefore, proceed to preach to them. Even St Paul himself did not begin with argument. It was repeatedly revealed to him
that he was called to preach to the Gentiles; but only after his action
had taken effect, when men disputed and opposed him, did he begin
to formulate a theory that results which he saw to be blessed were in
truth the fulfilment of Old Testament prophecies and teaching, and
a true revelation of the nature and work of Jesus Christ.

Thus the path by which the apostles reached the truth was sub-
missive obedience in act to the impulse of the Holy Spirit. When the
moment came, when the Spirit in them moved them to desire men's
salvation, and to feel their need, they acted, they spoke, they expressed that Spirit of love and desire, not knowing what the result of
their action might be, nor how to justify it intellectually, certain only
that they were directed by the Holy Spirit.

This seems to us very disturbing and dangerous. It looks like acting
upon the impulse of the moment. 'First act, then think,' sounds
strange doctrine in the ears of men like ourselves brought up to live
very much within the bounds of the proverb, 'Look before you leap.'
But there are two points at which men may look before they leap;
one without and one within, or one above and one below; and the

proverb suggests to us rather the outward and the below than the inward and the above. The apostles did not act thoughtlessly, because they did not base their action upon a nice calculation of the probable consequences. To calculate consequences and to act solely with a view to consequences, is worldly wisdom. The apostles were not guided in their action by worldly wisdom. They were guided by the Spirit. Care and wisdom are as clearly shown in consideration of the source as in consideration of the probable result of an action. It was this care and wisdom which the apostles showed. They did not consider .consequences so much as sources. The important question was not what result would follow, but from what source did the action spring. Persuaded that they were guided by the Spirit, they acted, and the result proved their wisdom.

This also was their defence when they were attacked. This was the ground upon which the whole body approved of the action of one of their number. When the Jews in Jerusalem disputed with St Peter concerning his action in going to the house of Cornelius, St Peter's answer was not to allay the anxiety of his opponents with regard to the possible consequences of his action, but to reassert the source of the action. He recounted his vision, he maintained that the Holy Spirit sent him, he declared that God gave the Holy Spirit to Cornelius and his household. His action was necessary. 'What was I, that I could withstand God?' (11.17). Convinced of the source of his action, the Council at once upheld it.

Similarly, St Paul defended his action before the Jerusalem Council. He had nothing to say of consequences possible or probable. He strove to convince his hearers that he had acted under the guidance of the Holy Spirit. To the apostles and elders he declared 'all things that God had done with them' (15.4); to the multitudes he declared 'what signs and wonders God had wrought among the Gentiles by them' (15.12). Signs and wonders were enough to prove to the multitude that God was with them; for all believed that 'no man can do these signs except God be with him.' The source of his action was more important than the probable consequences which worldly wisdom could foresee. When his hearers were convinced of the source of his action, opposition broke down. The leaders of the church accepted it and approved it.

Today we are more anxious about consequences, less sure of sources. When new and strange action is proposed, or actually effected, and questions are asked, the first question is, Is it wise? What will be the result of permitting such things to be done? We hear men argue, If we allow such and such actions to pass uncondemned the Church will have denied her faith, or her orders, or her sacraments, and the faith will be overthrown, the orders cease, the sacraments be destroyed. This was the sort of judgment which the apostles refused to admit. Only one other judgment is possible, and that is the judgment of the Spirit which led to the action. From this judgment the Church today shrinks. The Christian body does not seem to feel sure of its ground. Men say, We can judge actions: these are open. In judging these they seem to feel that they are dealing with something concrete. They feel at home with what they call facts; but the spirit which impelled the action seems to be something intangible and rather nebulous. They do not feel sure of themselves in dealing with that. If Christians take some unusual line of conduct and say, We felt impelled by the Spirit of God to do this, voices are heard on all sides, crying of precedents, and consequences. None seems to dare to inquire by what Spirit these men were impelled to their action. But this was the one question with which the apostles were wholly concerned in such a case.

When we turn from considerations of Spirit to considerations of policy and expediency we base our judgment upon the unknown; we forsake the way of the Spirit; we are in danger of losing the path which leads to the revelation of truth.

Of the results of action we are not capable judges. The Council of Jerusalem could not have foretold the results which would follow upon its decisions. St Paul himself could not foresee the results which would follow his journey to Jerusalem. Results are seldom exactly what we expect; they are often very different from our expectations. We assert boldly that such and such consequences will follow; they very seldom do. The man who anticipates with any approach to accuracy the consequences of any critical action is justly admired as a wonderful prophet. To base our judgment upon anticipation of consequences is to base it upon the most unstable foundations.

And the sure foundation we reject. Nowhere is the Spirit revealed as the Spirit who guides men by enabling them to anticipate the results of their action. Once and again the Spirit inspired prophets to foretell coming events so that the servants of God might prepare to take the right action when the event actually came to pass; never did

He cause men to foresee what the providence of God would cause to result from their action. But constantly, again and again, He inspired them to judge the spirit behind actions done. St Peter so judged the spirit of the lame man at the Beautiful Gate, and of Ananias and of Simon Magus; so Stephen judged the spirit of his opponents; so the apostles chose men full of the Holy Spirit; so St Paul judged the spirit which moved Elymas to oppose the conversion of the proconsul; and so the Council of Jerusalem judged the spirit which moved St Peter and St Paul when their actions seemed questionable. St John indeed exhorts Christians to try the spirits. In truth, this is the one thing that Christian men can judge. Spirit answers to spirit. Christian men inspired by the Holy Ghost can know the spirit which inspires such and such a man to do such and such an action. The Spirit was given to the Church that the Church might so judge spiritually spiritual things. To decline to question the spirit and to give our whole attention to the material form is to depart from the Spirit.

But it will perhaps be objected that we cannot be bound to approve every action which good men perform from high motives. Certainly we cannot. It is one thing to recognize that good men, moved by good motives, often do foolish, or even wrong, things; it is another to decline to appeal to the Spirit, preferring to base our judgments rather upon imagined consequences than upon recognition of spiritual guidance. Some actions are at once apparent: they could not be the result of the Holy Spirit's inspiration. Some are in doubt. It is these that we are to judge and to support or to oppose. My point is, that in arriving at a decision in a question of doubt, the apostles in the Acts were guided solely by their sense of the Spirit behind the action, not by any speculations as to consequences which might ensue.

And so they found the truth. Gradually the results of the action manifested themselves, and, seeing them, they perceived what they had really done, and learnt the meaning of the truth revealed in the action. But if, from fear of the consequences, they had checked or forbidden the action, they would have lost this revelation. They would have missed the way to truth. And that is the danger which besets judgments based upon expediency, or upon anticipations of results. Such judgments close the way to the revelation of new truth. The unknown is too fearful, the untried too dangerous. It is safer to refuse than to admit. So the possibility of progress is lost, and the opportunity. From this the apostles were saved by their recognition of the supremacy of the Spirit.

9

The Gift of the Spirit the Sole Test of Communion

Moved by the Holy Spirit given to them, the apostles went forth as missionaries. The Holy Spirit filled them with a desire for the salvation of men in Jesus Christ; He revealed to them the need of men. As they came into contact with different types and orders of men, so the Holy Spirit filled them with desire for the salvation of these and with the sense of their need. They could not but preach. Hence arose the great controversy over the admission of the Gentiles into the Church, a story which occupies so important a place in the Acts of the Apostles.

We have already seen how the apostles were led to preach to the Gentiles, how they justified their action on the ground that they were guided by the Holy Spirit. It now remains to point out how the church in Jerusalem was led to admit these Gentiles as members of the body.

The difficulty to be overcome was great. Before Christ came, a revelation of God had been made to men. One nation had been chosen by God to be the recipients of that revelation. The people of that nation had been brought near to Him. He had established His covenant with them. He had ordained the rites and ceremonies by which they should be admitted into His covenant and preserved in it. Christ, the Christ in whom the Apostles believed, whom they preached as the only Saviour, appeared in that nation, within that covenant. He came in fulfilment of promises made to the covenant people alone. He Himself accepted the authority of Moses, the great mediator of the covenant; He upheld the authority of the Mosaic system by word and by example. He obeyed the law, He observed the feasts. He learned the Scriptures, He quoted them with approval, He commanded obedience as a duty. Some traditional interpretations He rejected as calculated to overlay and hide the real force of the teaching contained in the Mosaic code; but no one, not even His enemies at His trial, contended that He broke the law, or undermined its authority, or that He attempted to lead men to despise, or to escape from, the covenant made by God with the fathers. He was condemned within the covenant on the ground that, within the covenant, He made a claim which His opponents declared to be blasphemous. Even St Paul, in his controversy with the Judaizing party within the Church, never attempted to argue that Christ in His life overtly, or by implication, had overthrown the law or had taught His disciples that they need not keep it.

Christ appeared within the covenant, and when He appointed His apostles He appointed only men who were within the covenant. He had found faith among Gentiles. Of one of these He had said that He had 'not found so great faith, no, not in Israel' (St Luke 7.9); but He called no Gentile to preach the gospel to Gentiles. He himself and His chosen Apostles were all within the covenant.

How, then, could disciples of this Christ do otherwise than He had done, or be other than He was? How could any one outside the covenant be the disciple of Christ who was within the covenant? The very notion was absurd. Could he be outside and inside at the same time? Could he follow a Christ who was within the covenant, whilst he remained outside the covenant? Could he accept Christ and not accept Moses whom Christ accepted? How could Christ's apostles overthrow the covenant, abandon the covenant themselves, and admit or recognize as servants of Christ men who were not within the covenant? Christ and His salvation were to be found only within the covenant. Who dare venture outside it? This argument alone should be sufficient to hinder any who called himself a Christian from preaching Christ without the law.

If such a dangerous experiment were tried, nothing but disaster could follow. The Mosaic teaching had been a preparation for the gospel invaluable and necessary. Outside the covenant what sort of ideas of God prevailed? The gods of the heathen were degraded and degrading abominations, devils, whose worship and everything connected with it was contamination for a righteous man. A few happily escaped out of the slough, but they escaped, not by listening to the teaching of philosophers, but by becoming proselytes. If, then, Gentiles were to become Christians, that was the path by which they must approach Christ.

If Gentile ideas of God needed to be corrected, their morals needed correction as fundamental. The immorality of the Phrygian scandalized the Greek; the immorality of the Greek scandalized the Roman of the old school; the immorality of them all scandalized the Jew still more deeply. Fornication was not even thought to be a vice. Men practised it openly, unashamed. It was not only condoned by religious men; it had a place in their religious rites. And vices more degrading still were commonly practised and condoned. Thus to the Jew the restrictions of the law were not merely valuable customs, designed to preserve the unity and purity of the people of God from contamination by intermixture with others, they were not merely safeguards of a ritual purity, they were the only possible and absolutely indispensable safeguards against positive and flagrant immorality. They were the foundation and pillar of sound moral life, both for the individual and for the people.

How, then, could the gospel be preached without the law? How could men accept Christ and not accept the law on which all purity of life depended? How could men be promised salvation in Christ without being directed to undergo the rite which symbolized adherence to the moral life, without being compelled to keep the law? Was immorality of life agreeable to Christian faith? Was Christ the minister of sin? Christ and holiness were inseparable. To teach men to believe in Christ, to teach them that they could be saved by Christ, without teaching tham the law was to separate these two. It was to ensure that the Christian faith would be divorced from purity of life.

To attempt to teach the heathen to keep the moral law without binding them to the Mosaic Law was to attempt the impossible. The Jews needed the law to direct them even at home; abroad they needed it still more. How, then, could new converts in an atmosphere of heathenism be expected to maintain any moral standard without the law? If they deliberately accepted the Jewish code, if they bore in their bodies the marks of their dedication to the moral life, if they associated themselves as closely as possible with those who, by tradition and inheritance and the long discipline of centuries of training, through much suffering had learnt the necessity of a high moral standard, then there was hope for them; but, without that, how could belief in Christ alone suffice? The temptations of their surroundings, the customs of their people, the inherited tendencies of ages would be too strong for them. They must fall. Christian morals would be no better than heathen morals. This was surely enough to secure that the Gentiles could never be admitted into the Church by Jews until they accepted circumcision and confessed themselves bound by the law.

But this was not all. If uncircumcised Gentiles were admitted into the Church what was to be their relation to faithful Jews? If Jews received them and shared with them in the Breaking of Bread, they themselves would lose their own position, they themselves would cease to be within the covenant, they would be unclean. For a keeper of the law to associate on equal terms with one who did not keep the law was impossible. Jewish Christians would, in accepting Gentiles, put themselves outside the pale. In order to admit men who, on every reasonable ground, ought not to be admitted, those who by birth and education were within must be exiled. What could be more absurd than to cast out the children in order to receive strangers who could never really be received, even at so great a price!

If the Jewish Christians received the uncircumcised they themselves and their children would lose the great safeguards which strict observance of the law provided. The weaker brethren would become worse than Grecian Jews. Already they had seen the dangers of laxity; they had seen a despised race of Jews who sought to compromise with heathen surroundings. Their history provided them with a fearful warning and a strong incentive to resist to the uttermost any approach to uncircumcised life. The story of the Maccabees might well deter them from weakness and persuade them to fight to the last for the strictest obedience to the law.

But even if they avoided the Gentile converts and refrained from communion with them, they could not escape. The mere fact that uncircumcised men were admitted into the Church, by whomsoever they might have been admitted and wherever, that mere fact that uncircumcised men were members of the Church of Christ would involve the acceptance of the principle that men could be saved without the law. The Church would be a body in which circumcised and uncircumcised members alike hoped for, and received, a like salvation. Then, if some men could be saved without the law, so could all. If the heathen who knew not the law could be saved by Christ in the Church, then the Jew too could be saved by Christ without the law, if he chose to abandon the law. The observance of the law was certainly a burden. Some, at least, would be glad to escape from the burden. Such an escape would be a great relief and a great con-

venience. Some would certainly escape. And so there would be Jewish
Christians living like heathen, and a great temptation to follow their
example would lie in the way of every young Christian who lived in
a Roman or Greek city. There was really no alternative. To admit
the uncircumcised meant that the Church of Christ forsook the
covenant rather than that the Gentiles were received into a church
within the covenant.

The example of Christ, the duty of disciples, the religious privileges
of the Jews, the foundations of morality, were all to be abandoned.
Any heathen who could show that he had been baptized might claim
to be in as good a position as the Jewish Christians. Surely it was absurd and wicked to suggest such a thing; and for what end was the
sacrifice to be made? Merely that heathen who were accustomed
to live licentious lives might escape from a burden which every Jew
and every proselyte knew that they ought to bear.

How was this argument answered? By one fact: God gave them
the Holy Spirit. 'They of the circumcision which believed were astonished, as many as came with Peter, because that on the Gentiles
also was poured out the gift of the Holy Ghost. For they heard them
speak with tongues, and magnify God. Then answered Peter, Can
any man forbid water, that these should not be baptized, which have
received the Holy Ghost as well as we?' (10.45-47). The gift of the
Holy Spirit to these men convinced and satisfied St Peter that they
must be received into the Church. When his action was called in
question at Jerusalem this was his answer: 'The Spirit bade me go
with them' (11.12); 'the Holy Ghost fell on them as on us at the beginning' (11.15); 'Forasmuch, then, as God gave them the like gift as
He did unto us who believed on the Lord Jesus Christ, what was I,
that I could withstand God?' (11.17). That answer silenced his opponents.

Later, when the preaching of St Paul and the rapid extension of
the Church in heathen provinces and the admission of large numbers
of men who had not even been taught the Jewish code caused the
question to be raised again, it was St Peter who, after hearing the account given by St Paul of his work, brought forward this first answer
to all objections. He simply recalled his own earlier experience. 'God,
which knoweth the hearts, bare them witness, giving them the Holy
Ghost, even as he did unto us' (15.8). If God gave the Holy Spirit
there was no more any possibility of refusal on the part of the apostles

to receive those to whom the Holy Ghost was given. No argument could stand in the face of that one fact.

The gift of the Holy Ghost is thus seen to be the one necessity for communion. If the Holy Ghost is given, those to whom He is given are certainly accepted in Christ by God. All who receive the Spirit are in reality and truth one. They are united by the strongest and most intimate of all ties. They are all united to Christ by His Spirit, and therefore they are all united to one another. Men may separate them, systems may part them from the enjoyment and strength of their unity; but, if they share the one Spirit, they are one.

In this case the new converts desired communion with the apostles. The apostles acknowledged that they had the Spirit. Being led themselves by the Spirit, they put aside all the countless and crushing objections which could be raised, they put aside all the serious disabilities under which these new converts laboured, they recognized the fact and accepted the consequence. God gave the Holy Spirit; they admitted at once that nothing more was needed for salvation, nothing else was needful for communion.

NOTES

1. Perhaps some one will say that all who were received into the Church by the apostles accepted the apostolic doctrine and order, none were admitted who did not accept these, and that consequently there is here another test of communion.

'To this I would answer: (1) The whole point of the story of Cornelius and of the admission of the Gentiles lies in the fact that these people had not accepted what up to that moment had been considered a necessary part of the Christian teaching. The question was whether they could be admitted without accepting the teaching and undergoing the rite. It was that question which was settled by the acknowledgment that they had received the Holy Spirit. (2) When the apostles spoke of men with whom they were not in communion, they used language which showed that they were convinced that those with whom they were not in communion had not the Spirit.[1] The moment it was admitted that they had the Spirit they were accepted.

The difficulty today is that Christians acknowledge that others have the Spirit, and yet do not recognize that they ought to be, and must be, because spiritually they are, in communion with one another. Men who hold a theory of the Church which excludes from communion those whom they admit to have the Spirit of Christ simply proclaim that their theory is in flat contradiction to the spiritual fact. Their theory separates those whom the Spirit unites. In other words, they and the Spirit differ on the question whether certain persons ought, or ought not, to be admitted to communion with Christ. The Spirit accepts them and dwells in them; the theory excludes them.

[1] In Jude 19 this is expressly stated. Many passages in St Paul's and St John's epistles manifestly imply it.

We must then distinguish carefully tests which prove whether the Spirit is given like St Paul's 'No man can say that Jesus is the Lord, but by the Holy Ghost' (1 Cor. 12, 3), and tests which are applied after it is admitted that the Holy Ghost is given. The first is a true test: for there can be no communion between those who have and those who have not the Spirit of Christ. The second is the introduction of a test to subvert a spiritual fact already acknowledged. This is exactly what the Acts of the Apostles teaches us not to do.

2. It will perhaps be said that in our present state of schism this assertion of spiritual principle can give us no definite guidance for action, can provide us with no clear programme, and must remain unfruitful. Surely that is not wholly true. It certainly must help us if we recognize that it is the presence of the Holy Spirit which creates a unity which we can never create. If men believe in the existence of this unity, they may begin to desire it, and desiring it to seek for it, and seeking it to find it. If, when they find it, they refuse to deny it, in due time, by ways now unsearchable, they will surely return to external communion.

It is not true that the assertion of spiritual principle is vain, because we cannot see at the moment how to express that principle in action. It would assuredly make a difference if Christians, in their approach one to another, realized that, in spite of appearances, they were in fact one. If, in their seeking after external reunion, they realized that they were seeking not to create a unity which does not yet exist, but to find an expression for a unity which does exist, which is indeed the one elemental reality, they would approach one another in a better frame of mind. The common recognition of the principle would in itself be a unifying force of great value, and would dispose those who shared it to approach questions of difference in a spirit of unity which would immensely assist their deliberations.

10

Conclusion

In the preceding chapters I have tried to show that the coming of the Holy Spirit at Pentecost was the coming of a missionary Spirit; that the Spirit stirred in the hearts of the disciples of Christ a great desire to impart that which they had received; that He revealed to them the need of men for that which He alone could supply; that He enabled them to hand on to others that which they themselves had received; that He led them to reach out farther and farther into the Gentile world, breaking down every barrier of prejudice which might have hindered their witness, or prevented them from receiving into communion men the most remote from them in habits of thought and life.

Those who received the Holy Spirit became witnesses. The gospel was spread not only by men set apart for this work, but also by the general body of disciples. After the death of Stephen 'they that were scattered abroad went everywhere preaching the word' (8.4); and the apostles are expressly excluded from the number of those who were so scattered (8.1). In Galatia, after St Paul's second visit, it is said that the churches were established in the faith, and increased in number daily (16.5). From Thessalonica 'the word of the Lord sounded, and not only in Macedonia and Achaia,' but far beyond (I Thess. 1.8). The whole history of the Church in the early centuries witnesses to the fact that the disciples were missionaries to the heathen among whom they lived.

The Spirit, the missionary Spirit, was given to all. Whosoever received the Holy Ghost received that, and, in some degree, if only by approval and support of the missionary efforts of others, expressed it. Some in the Church received special direction to special work in a special way or in particular places. So St Paul and Barnabas were called to evangelize the West. So St Peter was sent to the circumcision, so Timothy was taken from Lystra to help St Paul. Simeon and Niger and Manaen, and others like them, received no such special call. Yet they did not fail to manifest the missionary spirit within them.

The Spirit was given to all. Whosoever received the Holy Spirit in some degree, if only by approval and support of the efforts of others, expressed that desire for the conversion of the world which the Spirit inspired. What was wholly unknown, what was unthinkable in the early Church, was that Christians should oppose, or deride, or even fail to support, men who were labouring to spread the knowledge of Christ in the regions beyond. Not even the Judaizing party in Jerusalem did that. The Judaizers protested strongly against the form in which the gospel was preached to the Greeks; they sent out their own emissaries to attack, to undermine, and to destroy, so far as they possibly could, the influence and teaching of St Paul; but their opposition was directed, not against the conversion of the heathen, not against missionary work as such, but only against a particular form of teaching which they deemed to be dangerous. It was universally agreed that the gospel must be preached to all the nations.

All who received the Spirit were more or less conscious of the missionary impulse of the Spirit. They all truly obeyed the command to go into all the world, for they all possessed a Spirit which impelled them to desire the world-wide manifestation of Christ. And it is the world-embracing Spirit which obeys the command rather than the wandering body. Christ came into all the world, though in the flesh He never went outside Palestine. It is obviously necessary to avoid the mistake of thinking that the reception and expression of the missionary Spirit necessarily involves going on missionary journeys, or that missionary journeys are necessarily truer and fuller expressions of the missionary Spirit than any other. The Spirit of redeeming love is manifestly expressed as truly in striving for the salvation of men at home as in preaching to the heathen beyond the seas. It is the reception and the expression of redeeming love which is of importance, rather than the manner or the form of the work in which that Spirit is expressed.

The Spirit of desire for the salvation of the world may be expressed in any form of Christian activity; but that Spirit is not revealed to others with equal clearness by every form of activity. In the Acts, as I have tried to point out, St Luke makes the revelation of the Spirit clear to us by setting before us the acts of those men in the early Church whose lives were devoted to what we, today, call 'missionary work. If he had dwelt upon the labours of those others who were not engaged in this special missionary work the revelation would have been less clear. The work of those who organized the Church may well have been as true an expression of the Spirit of redeeming love as the work of those of whom St Luke tells us most; but if he had written at length of church organization we should probably have missed the revelation of the Spirit as the Spirit which labours for the salvation of the world. When, by the insistence of St Luke upon the missionary aspect, we have learnt to know the Spirit as the Spirit who inspires active zeal for the salvation of others, we can then easily perceive the same Spirit in other forms of activity, and we can understand that the organization of the church and the amelioration of social conditions are equally forms in which that Spirit finds expression. We then find that every form of Christian activity may be used to express that Spirit. Every form of work can be undertaken in that Spirit, each individual finding in his own proper work the best way to manifest that desire for the salvation of men which the Holy Spirit inspires.

In this large sense, if we believe in the Holy Spirit as He is revealed in the Acts, we must be missionaries. We cannot accept the teaching of the Acts, we cannot believe that the one thing of importance to our souls is to receive and to know the Spirit, without feeling ourselves driven to missionary action. We cannot believe that the Holy Spirit reveals our own need and the need of men without beginning to feel that need of men for Christ laid upon us as a serious call to action. We cannot believe that the Holy Spirit is given to us that those who so need Christ may be by us brought to find the one way of salvation for their souls and bodies in this world and in the world to come, without feeling impelled to action. We cannot believe that men everywhere, whatever their previous education or ignorance, whatever their civilization or barbarism, are capable of receiving Christ and His salvation, without being moved to take a world-wide view of our responsibility. We must embrace the world because Christ embraces the world, and Christ has come to us, and Christ in us embraces the world. Activity world-wide in its direction and intention and hope and object is inevitable for us unless we are ready to deny the Holy Spirit of Christ revealed in the Acts.

93

III

THE
VOLUNTARY
CLERGY

The Case for Voluntary Clergy (1930) is now rather rare. It incorporated the substance of two earlier volumes — *Voluntary Clergy* (1923) and *Voluntary Clergy Overseas* (1928) — and also of the pamphlet *Mission Activities* (2nd edition, 1930). Twelve of the original twenty-two chapters were included in *The Ministry of the Spirit* (1960). The selections included here are chapters 3, 4, 5, 7, 8, and 10 of this shortened version.

11

Vocation

Nowhere in the Bible do we find that men were invited to offer themselves for the priesthood. In the Old Testament the example of Korah was presented as a warning: the priesthood was given to a family chosen by God through Moses. In the New Testament we hear nowhere of men being invited to offer themselves for any office in the church. The apostles did not offer to be apostles, the seventy did not offer themselves, St Matthias did not offer himself, the seven deacons in the Acts did not offer themselves: in no church of apostolic foundation was there any suggestion that anyone was appointed because he offered himself. In the Pastoral Epistles, Timothy and Titus were not told to invite men to offer themselves.[1]

In the Old Testament it is true that prophets obeyed an inward and direct call to speak in God's name, but that was not a vocation to offer themselves for the position of officers in the church. In the New Testament and in the early Church, apparently some of the evangelists and some of the prophets obeyed a purely inward vocation to preach Christ, but that was not a vocation to accept the office of a deacon or of a priest—still less an office to which a stipend was attached. To apply these examples to the case of men who are asked to seek offices of dignity and emolument in the church is to misuse them. The call of Isaiah is often taken as a test to urge young men to offer themselves for Holy Orders; but Isaiah did not offer himself for a priesthood and a stipend.

Vocation to the ministry of the church has two sides. If it is important that a man should be convinced that he is called by God to serve, it is also of importance that the church which he is to serve should be convinced that he is the best man to serve it. Now if we set out to establish the church in every little group of communicants all over the world we should recover the reality of the local church, and with that we should recover once more that side of vocation which we have lost. The local church would be compelled to consider who were the best men to serve from among its own members. It

---

[1] 'If a man desire' does imply that there were men eager to be appointed; but that is quite a different matter from appealing to men to offer.

would be incredible folly to invite anyone who liked to offer himself, as if the office could be filled by anybody. The local church must be led by men whom it respected and whose services it would accept. Many of the best men would decline to put themselves forward. They know that to fulfil the office they must have the moral support of their congregation, and that it would be fatal to open the door to the jibe that they were putting themselves on a pedestal. The church would be driven to propose the men: the bishop would certainly take counsel with the body of the communicants, and when he was sure that the best men in the group were before him he would solemnly call upon those men to serve. The call so presented would be a vocation which no one could doubt or deny.

Under our present system we still retain some hints and relics of that external vocation, but the appeal to young men to offer themselves for ordination has so obscured the reality of it that it is practically lost. The young man is invited to offer himself before the church has called him; and he is expected to know and be sure of his vocation before one half of it exists. Were the call of the church put first, the internal vocation could respond to that. If the man was internally convinced that the call of the church through the mouth of the bishop did not express to him the call of God, if he were internally aware that a mistake was being made, if his secret knowledge of his own life and character assured him that he was not a proper person to serve, he could refuse to do so; if, on the other hand, he recognized that he ought to fulfil the duty he would accept it. He might, indeed, believe that he was the best man to serve before the call came to him, and he might wish to be chosen; but that would not justify him in offering. The two sides of vocation ought to correspond to make a true vocation. Then all doubt is removed.

Some men say that this is pure congregationalism, but it is nothing of the sort. The congregation does not simply elect its ministers. The presence and action of the bishop make all the difference. The call of God is established through His church. If bishops appealed to men of goodwill; if they went to the place and told the congregation the plain truth: 'You know quite well that you cannot have a stipendiary minister; I have not the men and you have not the money'—if they asked them, 'Have you not here two or three men fit to serve who between them could lead the church and minister the sacraments: men whose ministration you will accept?' often they would be answered: 'Yes, we have.' And if the bishops then solemnly and openly put it to those men: 'It is your duty to do this service: in the name of Christ and in the name of the church I demand that you shall serve,' not many men would refuse.

But it is objected that such men would be untrained, and that under our present system we can persuade young men that they have a vocation and then train them. To that I must answer that this conception of training is, like our conception of vocation, one-sided. If we read the instructions given to Timothy and Titus in the Pastoral Epistles, and consider the qualifications there laid down for the ministry of the Church, we see at once that the apostolic writer lays great stress on the training upon which we lay very little, and scarcely hints at the training on which we lay so much. The training on which the apostolic writer lays the greatest stress is the training which God alone can give, the training of life and experience; the training on which we lay the greatest stress is the training that *we* can give, the training of the school or the college. The training on which we lay stress is the training which is suited to the young; but God does not call only the young to be his ministers. Men are not only converted to Christ in youth: they are converted often late in life and, in the apostolic conception, they are generally called to the ministry of the church after years of experience. The training on which we lay stress is almost wholly intellectual; the training on which the apostle laid stress is almost wholly spiritual and practical. The training upon which we lay stress is comparatively superficial; the training on which the apostle laid stress is vital and fundamental.

Our conception of the relationship between the clergy and those to whom they minister is one sided. We always look at the matter from this point of view: Here are so many parishes, here are so many clergy; if there are not enough clergy for the parishes then there are still only so many clergy, and they must be sent to the parishes which, for one reason or another, seem to be the most important. But surely that is not the true way of looking at the matter; surely we ought to say: Here is a group of Christian people: this group of Christians must be properly organized with its own clergy; the only question before us is, Who ought to serve this group? If a suitable man is willing to go there and they are willing to receive his ministrations, well and good; but, if not, they must still have clergy, and the only question is, Who are the men who ought to serve them?

The responsibility for their religious life must rest upon them. If they decline to take any interest in the matter, then we cannot make them take a proper interest by sending someone to minister to them; when they do not want church life, we cannot make church life simply by sending a man to hold a service. Something far more fundamental than that is needed. A man may go to them as a visitor and urge upon them the importance of church life, but he cannot create it by going to minister to them when he knows, and they know, that at any moment he may go away, and the church life will thereupon cease. If the people really desire to live in the church, then it ought to be made possible for them to do so. In other words, we must think first and foremost of the group as the church in the place, and of the ministers as naturally and normally members of that group, attached to it by every tie, spiritual and social. When we put the church first and see that the clergy come out of the church (and I am speaking of the church in that local sense), then at once we recover the family aspect of the church. The church is at once a local entity as certain and clear and distinct as the village or the group, and we escape at once from that imperfect loose relationship of cleric and people which finds expression in such terms as 'We will starve him out' and 'He does not belong to us', for those expressions are a sore weakness.

12

The Meaning and Place of Voluntary Clergy

Voluntary clergy are men who earn their living by the work of their hands or of their heads in the common market, and serve as clergy without stipend or fee of any kind.

(1) Since stipendiary clergy are voluntary in one sense and voluntary clergy are only opposed to stipendiary in another, we ought not to oppose them as if one excluded the other. It must be plain to anyone who has read my chapter on the apostolic qualifications that I did not there attempt to prove that the clergy should never be paid. The apostolic qualifications are quite compatible with dependence for livelihood upon the offerings of the faithful, either in the form of endowments, or of subscriptions. The means by which the minister gains his living is not in the picture. He may earn it by a trade, or inherit wealth from his ancestors, or enjoy a salary, or receive dues as an official, or be supported by the church. How he is supported is a mere external detail, which is not even mentioned. His call of God and his service do not depend upon such things as that.

The church unquestionably needs some men who give themselves wholly to prayer and the ministration of the Word and Sacraments, and such men must be supported by the faithful. She needs also some men whose time is wholly occupied with the care of parishes, and these she must maintain. She needs also scholars who give their whole time to study, and these she must maintain. But there are countless small groups of Christians needing pastors, which cannot afford to maintain clergy nor to provide them with sufficient occupation to save them from the temptations of idleness. There are also many large town parishes where the church needs assistant priests of varied capacity, drawn from many classes of the people, who can speak, each to his own class, in the language familiar to it, understanding by experience the difficulties and temptations of that class. It is also important that many services and sermons should not be heaped upon one man: the stipendiary ought to be able to leave his parish at proper intervals for rest and refreshment without feeling that his people are neglected and his work left undone; he ought also to be relieved from a pressure which drives him to minister when he is sick and unfit. It is in such cases that the assistance of voluntary clergy would be invaluable.

(2) The ordination of such men would give no additional excuse to anyone to question the disinterestedness of the stipendiary clergy. Men sometimes think that voluntary clergy would appear to be disinterested labourers for love, whilst the stipendiary clergy would be thought to be hirelings, and that invidious comparisons would be made. But all men know that those who give up their whole time to a particular work must have the wherewithal to live. Every one would know that the work of a stipendiary cleric precluded his labouring in the market. Every one would know that the work of the stipendiary was not the work of the voluntary cleric. All sensible men would know that the church needs both. The argument that the ordination of voluntary clerics would lead men to question the disinterestedness of the stipendiary is very weak. If men questioned it then, it would be because they question it now. Disinterestedness is not proved by the exclusion of voluntary workers. Wherever it is, there it makes itself felt; and it does not manifest itself by building a hedge round itself. Men do not question the disinterested zeal of paid prison visitors because there are many unpaid visitors: they do not question the disinterested zeal of paid secretaries of philanthropic societies, because there are many unpaid secretaries. They question disinterestedness only when the conduct of the stipendiary suggests that he is more concerned about securing his own position than he is about the cause for which he works.

The ordination of voluntary clergy would not cause men to question the disinterestedness of the stipendiary clergy: it would indeed enlighten them, because they would escape from that confusion between vocation to serve and a means of livelihood of which I spoke in the previous chapter. If once men saw that vocation to serve was not necessarily vocation to a certain means of earning a livelihood, they would distinguish between vocation and livelihood, and they would understand vocation, and they would respect it in all in whom they saw its fruits. Thus the ordination of voluntary clergy, so far from bringing the service of stipendiary clergy into disrepute, would exalt it; because the stipend would drop into its proper place as a mere accident, and vocation to serve would stand out clearly in its purity. The difficulty which we have been considering arises not from the presence of voluntary clergy, but from their absence. Men question the disinterestedness of the clergy because they make stipends a necessity, something without which there can be no clergy, something without which they themselves would not be clergy. That is the real difficulty. If once we disabused men's minds of that idea by producing clergy who had no stipends this cause of misunderstanding would be taken away.

(3) Neither would the existence of voluntary clergy undermine the liberality of the laity. Clerics often say that if voluntary clergy were admitted, the laity would cease to support stipendiary clergy, and that they would say, We can get clergy for nothing, why should we pay for them? That argument suggests that the laity do not want stipendiary clergy and must be compelled to have them against their will. Whatever truth there may be in it, and it is a very serious indictment of the present stipendiary clergy as a body, one thing is certain, we cannot make people want what they do not want by compelling them to pay for it.

Suppose that our bishops ordained voluntary clergy. We all know that we must have some men who give up all other means of earning their livelihood: if we do not, we should very quickly find it out. Then we must support them, and, knowing our need of them, we should support them without any entreaty. If all the work which could be done by men earning their own living were done by men earning their own living, much work which now falls upon one man and prevents him from earning his own living could easily be performed by three or four men, all of whom could earn their own living, and all the necessary stipendiary clergy could be easily maintained.

Would that undermine the liberality of the laity? Is there no liberality in service, or is liberality shown only in subscribing money? That is a strange notion of liberality which confines it to the offering of money only.

(4) The distinction between stipendiary and voluntary clergy is not a distinction between men who give their whole time to the service of God and His church and men who give part of their time to that service, but a distinction between one form of service and another. Both stipendiary and voluntary clergy ought to be serving God and the Church all the time in all they do; but the service

which the Church needs that each should do for God and for her is not the same. The voluntary cleric carries the priesthood into the market place and the office. It is his work not only to minister at the altar or to preach, but to show men how the common work of daily life can be done in the spirit of the priest.

In the mission field this want of experience is even more serious than it is at home; because here at home so much of our life is intellectual, whereas there the majority of our converts have very little intellectual experience. Their life is wholly built on practical experience, and what they need in a leader is someone who can understand and appreciate, and speak in terms of that practical experience. All those whom they naturally recognize as leaders are men who have learned wisdom in this school of practical experience. But the church scarcely ordains any who have not been trained from youth in mission schools. Consequently, in the mission field the first converts can have no ministers of their own until boys have been educated in schools. Then these boys are sent as teachers first, then as catechists, and finally as priests, without any real experience of the life of the people whom they are to lead, to guide and direct a congregation composed of mature and experienced men. Thus the organization of the church is delayed in a most unhealthy way, and the clerical order is established on a most unhealthy basis, whilst the natural leaders of the Christian people are suppressed, and put into a very false position.

Among our own people also the church sorely needs clergy in close touch with the ordinary life of the laity, living the life of ordinary men, sharing their difficulties and understanding their trials by close personal experience. Stipendiary clergy cut off by training and life from that common experience are constantly struggling to get close to the laity by wearing lay clothing, sharing in lay amusements, and organizing lay clubs; but they never quite succeed. To get close to men, it is necessary really to share their experience, and to share their experience is to share it by being in it, not merely to come as near to it as possible without being in it. The church needs clerics who really share the life of their people. The life of the voluntary cleric is not divorced from the life of the laity, it is the life of the laity lived as a cleric ought to live it.

(5) That is why I shudder when I hear men talk of voluntary clergy as half-timers. Voluntary clergy are not half-timers. A cleric

can no more be a half-time cleric than a father can be a half-time father, or a baptized Christian a half-time Christian. Our present clerics are not half-time clerics, though a very large part of their time is often spent in social or financial business. Some of them, for instance the clerical secretary of a society like the Society for the Promotion of Christian Knowledge, are engaged all day long in business which might very well be performed by secular officers, but they do not cease to be clerics on that account, nor become half-time clerics. A priest is not a priest only when he is performing strictly priestly offices. We cannot divide life into two compartments, one secular and the other religious, and say that a cleric must only be engaged in those acts which we put outside the secular division. We often talk like that; but in practice it is impossible, and in principle it is false. Such a division is utterly opposed to the teaching of the New Testament. For Christian men all work is Christ's, not part of it; all life is Christ's; He claims the whole of it. Yet the habit of dividing life into sacred and secular compartments is so ingrained in us that Christian priests, who preach the true doctrine and themselves are constantly engaged in what is, in common speech, purely secular work, see nothing inconsistent with their doctrine when they speak of voluntary clergy as half-timers, or oppose their ordination on the ground that they will be too much occupied with secular business.

There can be no such thing as secular business for a Christian man, if by 'secular' is meant 'not religious.' In exactly the same sense there can be no secular work for a man called by God to the sacred ministry of the Church. He has a profession in a very different sense from that in which we commonly speak of the ministerial profession. We speak of the ministerial profession, as men speak of the legal profession, as a means by which a man earns his livelihood. But that is not the true sense in which a priest has a profession. A priest has a profession in the sense in which every baptized person has a profession.

In our Baptismal Service we are told that 'Baptism doth represent unto us our profession, which is to follow our Saviour Christ and to be made like unto him.' That is a purely spiritual conception of profession. It does not depend at all upon the means of livelihood of the baptized. He may be tinker, or tailor, or physician, or lawyer. Whatever his means of livelihood may be, he is bound by that profession. He can follow his Saviour Christ in any walk of life and be made like unto Him. His profession covers all types of work and includes all the acts of life. The whole life is bound up and unified in it. Whatever the baptized may be doing at any time and in any place he is bound by that profession. He cannot be bound by it in one set of circumstances and not bound by it in another set of circumstances.

Just so ordination represents a profession; and I think that it ought to represent a profession always in this sense. It represents a profession of a divine call to minister to Christ's people, a spiritual profession, independent of all material circumstances. The baptized is always baptized: the priest is always a priest. He can never escape from that priesthood, any more than a baptized person can escape from his baptism. The whole life is unified in this profession, as in that. It matters not what the priest may be doing externally at any particular moment. He is not a priest only when he is in church celebrating the holy mysteries: he is a priest always, everywhere, He is not bound by his profession only in one set of circumstances and not bound by it in a different set of circumstances. His profession is independent of the external circumstances, though it may be more apparent to the world in some circumstances than in some others. A minister of Christ is one whom God has called to bear in his person the character of a man called by God to minister always under all circumstances.

(6) The difference between voluntary clergy and stipendiary clergy is not the difference between qualified and unqualified men, but between different types of qualification. When men speak of voluntary clergy they often say that they would be unqualified. That is a mistake. They would be fully qualified, as fully qualified as the stipendiary, but differently. It is hard to think that any one who reads the qualifications laid down in the Pastoral Epistles, which I discussed above, could say that the man who possessed them was unqualified: yet that is what we hear today. We are so enamoured of those qualifications which we have added to the apostolic that we deny the qualifications of anyone who possesses only the apostolic, whilst we think a man fully qualified who possesses only ours. A young student fresh from a theological college lacks many of those qualifications which the apostle deemed necessary for a leader in the house of God, the age, the experience, the established position and reputation, even if he possesses all the others. Him we do not think unqualified. The man who possesses all the apostolic qualifications is said to be unqualified, because he cannot go back to school and pass an examination.

(7) Voluntary clergy are not men who simply occupy the position of the present stipendiary without his stipend.

In speaking of voluntary clergy we ought to think more of the church than of the clergy, and we ought to seek not so much for suitable men from the point of view of the clerical order as for suitable groups to be established as churches. We ought to think of the ordination of voluntary clergy as the proper way to establish the group as a church. A suitable group is a group of communicants: the suitable men are the men whose ministrations the group will accept. Such men are suitable ministers for that group, at its present stage of development. The apostolic qualifications then apply. A group which suggested that it should be constituted as a church by the ordination of men who had not the apostolic qualifications would prove that it was not a suitable group; but I think that such a group of Christians would rarely be found. The establishment of churches with voluntary clergy is a very different matter from seeking for individuals to recruit a body of clerics.

Again, I have found men trying to imagine a voluntary cleric in the position of the present stipendiary, and saying that it is impossible. That is because they were thinking of one man in sole charge of a parish, overseas, of an enormous parish. The apostolic voluntary clergy were not isolated individuals in charge of parishes. The apostles always ordained several clergy for each place; and if we returned to their practice today, voluntary clergy would certainly not be put in the position of the present stipendiary. Where there was a stipendiary cleric the voluntary clerics would support him; and sickness, holidays, resignations, removals, of the stipendiary, would cause no interruption of the regular life of the church. Instead of being ruled by one man, every church would be led by a college of priests who between them would be responsible for the due conduct of the services and the proper direction of the church. Where there was no stipendiary cleric, there would still be a sufficient number of voluntary clerics to maintain all the proper services of the church.

It has been said that the appointment of voluntary clergy 'is a question exclusively for the exercise of the episcopal judgment.'[1] I venture to say that is a serious mistake. We must remember that in countless instances the choice is not between stipendiary clergy and voluntary clergy but between voluntary clergy and none at all: we

[1] *World Call*, vol. v., p. 27.

must remember that everywhere it is a question whether the church is to be adequately served. Whether Christian men are or are not to be deprived of their church life and taught to do without it, whether the church is to be adequately supplied with ministers, are questions not only for episcopal judgment, but for the judgment of all good men. The assertion that the ordination of voluntary clergy is a question exclusively for the exercise of the episcopal judgment is a typical example of that terrible division of the Church to which Bishop Mandell Creighton referred when he said: 'The Church is divided into two bodies, one offering, the other accepting Christian privileges.'[1]

---

[1] *Life and Letters*, vol. II, p. 375.

13

Why?

I went one day into a synod office in Canada. I found there two men: the one was a young theological student, the other a man of about fifty years of age who told me that for fifteen years, when he was farming on the prairie, he held services in his own house for his neighbours. At first some six or seven Anglicans came, but later some of the other people came also. They had a celebration of the Holy Communion two or three times a year when a priest passed that way.

I looked at those two men and I could not help asking myself why the bishop was going to ordain the one and why he had not ordained the other. If spiritual experience is desirable for a priest, which of those two men had the largest spiritual experience? If intellectual ability was considered, I had no doubt which of the two was the abler man: if education, a very short conversation revealed which of them was the better educated. If it is important that a parish priest should be able to lead and direct his congregation, who could question for a moment which of those two men most commanded respect? Which of them had the best and strongest social influence? The one was a married man, and his wife and children were respected in the society in which they lived: the other was unmarried and no one could foretell whom he would marry or whether his wife would be a help or a hindrance to him in his work. The diocese was understaffed, and appealing incessantly for aid in money and in men: which of these men would be the greatest burden on its scanty funds? The one was being supported as a student, and must be supported by the diocese as long as he lived, unless he went away or committed some flagrant offence: the other never had, and never would, cost the diocese a halfpenny. The one lived up-country for fifteen years, and during all that time lacked nothing but Orders to be the pastor of his flock: he would undoubtedly have built up the church where he lived. Of the other all that could be said was that he was apparently a very respectable young man; whether he would be a leader of men, or a good parish priest, when he was forty years of age; whether he would stay more than a year or two doing up-country work; whether he would

not soon be seeking a town parish, or desiring one, which would
equally distract his mind from the work up-country, even if it did not
result in his leaving it, who could foretell? Every one hoped for the
best, but no one could be certain. All these possibilities made his
training and ordination (from the point of view of a diocese which
needed above all things the church built up in small scattered groups)
a pure gamble with the funds at the disposal of the diocese. No one
could be sure how he would turn out. About the elder man there was
not a shadow of doubt; he was no novice, he had approved himself.

Why then did the bishop not ordain that man when he was on his
farm doing exactly the work which the church needed? Why did he
leave him unequipped and hampered by lack of ordination? And
why was he determined to ordain only the younger man? It is not as
though he said: The diocese needs both, and I shall ordain both. No.
He said: I cannot ordain the one whom every group of Christians
would naturally think the better and more suitable man; I shall ordain the younger with all the uncertainties which surround him, and
I shall ordain the younger only. Why did he do that? I asked men
that question, but I got no answer.

If we look at the history of any society which has spread and
grown in the world, what do we see? Do we not see that it has grown
because members of the society have scattered and have carried with
them the ideas and practices which the society was founded to maintain? Do we not see the members creating new branches of the society
wherever they go? They think that the society to which they belong
is a good society, and they invite others to join it: they band themselves together wherever they find two or three fellow members and
strengthen one another. They hold meetings, they practise their doctrine, whatever it may be. They appeal to the parent society for
recognition as a true branch of the society: they are enrolled, and
their branch is enrolled as a branch of the society.

Is not that the way in which all societies, religious, social, or
political, grow? Look at the progress in modern days of Theosophical
societies, of Christian Science, of Trade Unionism, of Islam, of
Masonry—is it not in that way that they have made progress? Look
at the early Church; was it not in that way that it spread all over the
Roman Empire, and beyond it?

There was indeed this difference between the expansion of the
Church and the expansion of a secular society: that in place of a for-

mal enrolment of a new branch in the archives of a head office, the Church recognized and established new churches by a spiritual act, the solemn ordination of ministers for the new churches, but that did not hinder the expansion; it assisted it.

Suppose we saw a society which insisted that officers must be sent from the head office to direct and manage every new branch: should we not be surprised, and should we not ask how such a society could possibly expand widely? We should probably conclude that the society in question was anxious rather to check than to encourage any rapid advance. We should probably imagine that the society observed some esoteric mystery of so difficult and strange a character that its ordinary members could not be trusted to teach or to practise it, and that the society was far more anxious to preserve the purity of this esoteric mystery than to admit new members. We should conclude that it was not a society designed to admit many, nor anxious to enlarge its borders by the creation of new branches. And if we were told that as a matter of fact the mystery was a very simple rite designed for the use of even illiterate members, and that the society was one which proposed to conquer the whole world, and was eager to see as many branches as possible established, should we not then be utterly nonplussed?

But that is what we see in the church today. We see Christian churchmen who might be, and ought to be, the founders of new churches scattered all over the world, some of them eager to extend the church; but they are carefully taught that they must not practise their religion. If there is anywhere an isolated group of Christians today, they can have no church life, they cannot live as members of a Church in which the rites of Christ are observed, unless they can get one of the ordained class to come to them; for no bishop ordains one or two of them to act for their fellows as the bishops of the early Church did. All natural expansion ceases. The scattered laity are impotent.

Again we ask why is this? It is not a light matter. The scattered members of the church upon whose practice of their religion increase and progress naturally depend are very numerous. The world is sprinkled with such groups. No one who knows anything at all about the facts imagines that we ever have sent, or are now sending, enough clergy to provide for all these groups. Why then do not bishops act now as bishops acted in the years when the church was expanding throughout the Roman Empire? The answer unquestionably is that a long established tradition decrees that the clergy must be an order apart, a professional body of men who engage in no other work than their clerical work, and, unless they have private means, wholly dependent for their livelihood upon their clerical profession. Small groups cannot produce such men and cannot support them: therefore they cannot be established.

The tradition is certainly not primitive; it certainly restricts the expansion of the church; it certainly runs counter to the direct commands of Christ, but it is accepted as gospel by all our bishops and by most of our laity. It has so strong a hold upon the church that it is scarcely ever questioned. Again and again in Canada and in Africa and in India I have seen men taken completely by surprise when I suggested that there was no valid reason why a bishop should not ordain a good Christian to minister to his fellows whilst yet he continued to earn his livelihood by his accustomed trade or profession. They could scarcely believe their ears.

It is this tradition which makes the establishment of the church a matter of finance. This is the difference between the establishment of the church in early days and the establishment of the church now. In those days the establishment of the church was a spiritual operation, today it is a financial operation. That is no hasty exaggerated statement. In those days it was a matter of prayer and laying on of hands: now it is a matter of raising a stipend.

Put in that crude form, which is nevertheless the true form in actual fact, as we see it today, we might even begin to doubt whether such a restraint, a restraint which makes the existence of a church depend upon money, is not farther removed from the truth of the gospel than the practice which insists that the Christians are the Church and must live and act as a church even without episcopally ordained ministers.

There is at least here an equality. Natives of India or of Africa or of China sometimes think that we do not establish the Church among them because we despise them, or think them too ignorant or uncivilized to be ordained. They think sometimes that here is the taint of the colour bar, because we ordain so few nationals. But that is not true. I have said to them: Our bishops treat our own people exactly as they treat you. They say that our own settlers are too ignorant to celebrate the Lord's Supper: they say that they can have no ordered church life unless they can import a young cleric from England to look after them. They treat all alike in this.

All over the world is scattered a multitude of groups of Christians, and a daily increasing number, which depend for any church life upon a foreign source of supply. That is our conception of the way in which the church ought to be established. It is supposed that as the groups grow in wealth they will be able and willing to support a professional minister. That sometimes actually happens; and because it happens in some places, the miserable state of the places in which it does not happen, and the loss which takes place whilst it is coming to pass, is forgotten.

The *World Call*, after speaking of parishes '100 miles from the centre in every direction,' of 'groups never yet visited,' of 'a celebration perhaps once a year,' of 'a week's journey if the settler is to attend a service' and such like cases, with which it says that its 'reports are full,' concludes: 'If no means are found to supply the needs of these impossible parishes, it is inevitable that many people must lapse.'[1]

---

[1] *World Call*, vol. v., p.26.

14

Desertion Unnecessary

I suggest that there is only one way in which we can meet this need:
I am persuaded that the church could meet the situation if only
she would shake herself free from the tradition which may once have
been useful in England but is now but a yoke upon our necks,
shackles upon our feet. We must distinguish between settled officers
of the church, who are necessary for its local organized life, and
evangelists or teachers, who wander about from place to place to
convert the indifferent or to stir and encourage the members of the
settled churches. We must distinguish between those two classes of
ministers. It is the duty of the settled local officers to direct the
affairs of the local church and to see that her services are regularly
and properly conducted: their first care and duty is the local church
in which they live. The missionary, on the other hand, is essentially
a wandering evangelist or teacher, and therefore he cannot be the
pastor of a settled church; because he cannot both move about and
be always at hand to serve the church in which he lives. The local
clergy of the church must be resident and there must be enough of
them in every little local church to make sure that the church is
never without its proper ministers. They must have their proper
occupation by which they earn their daily bread, and that for two
reasons: firstly, that most of these little groups could not afford to pay
them, even if they wanted to do so, and, secondly, that if the clergy
had nothing but clerical work to do, in little tiny groups they would
not have enough to keep them occupied.

Now the moment that we make that distinction, and put the
question of pay out of our minds, we can see at once that the church
could be established in every little group throughout the whole
world. Wherever there were church people who desired to live in an
organized church and to enjoy all its privileges and its sacraments,
there the church could be at once established. When I suggested that
the only possible way of establishing the church in a wide area north
of Winnipeg was to send men to seek out the good communicants
among the people and then to ordain these as voluntary clergy, so
that the lamp of the church would be permanently alight in at least

some of the townships, and an example set to every group and a way opened to them by which they obviously could, if they would, secure for themselves a regular church life, the baptism of their children, and the administration of the Holy Communion, I was told at once of men at two places who would be well fitted to serve. Now, if we began with those two places, if voluntary priests were ordained there, the candle of the church would be lighted in the very heart of the great neglected area.

If the missionary had no local church to care for; if it was his business to go up and down the country striving to convert men to Christ and to bring them to realize that they could have the fullest church life the moment that they were willing to receive it; if wherever they heard his message the church was established, two things would inevitably follow: firstly, settlers who desired church life, seeing that it was at hand, seeing that they could enjoy it if they would, and that there was nothing to hinder them if they would serve, would realize their power. There are many, very many, good church people scattered about the world who would respond, and wherever they responded, there the church would be. Secondly, the missionary, being no longer bound to minister to settled groups, would be able to proceed from place to place over a very wide area, and his success would consist not in finding a group which would restrain his further progress, but in establishing a church from which he could make a further advance. If the members of any group over the widest areas had not, in a very short time, a full church life, it would be entirely their own fault, because such a system would supply the need of every group that wanted church life. Working on that apostolic order, every group in the world could have its full church life.

It is no answer to me to say that there are many groups which would not at once respond. My point is that there are some now ready, and that we waste our missionary clergy in taking services for those who could best do without them, to the neglect of those who most need them. If we began to establish churches with voluntary clergy, every church so established would make it more easy for the missionary to extend his labours. When the apostles began their work in Europe they did not find groups of nominal Christians with centuries of Christian life behind them, all able to read, with the whole Bible in their possession. Yet they could so establish churches with their proper ministers that they had no need to remain to hold services for them. We today, starting with that great initial advantage, might surely follow their example. All that is necessary is to break a tradition that Christians must wait for a cleric to come from some distant source to minister to them. If we began at once where men are prepared to welcome the opportunity, we should both set free missionaries for pioneer work and we should have entered upon a path by which every group in the world could be established; and all men would see it. The door would be open for every group of Christian churchmen in the world to enjoy full church life. It is no answer to say that some groups are not ready to respond to an appeal which they have never heard.

15

Itinerant Clergy

B ecause we use missionary clergy to do the work of parish priests we are compelled to spread their services thin. All over the world I see clergy itinerating over wide areas, ministering to three, or four, or a dozen, or twenty congregations.

These congregations under one priest and theoretically composing one parish are distinct congregations often remote from one another. They do not know one another, they cannot recognize any unity among themselves as a parish. Consequently the parish has no real, living unity in itself: it has only a nominal and fictitious unity. No such parish can act as one unit. The moment that anything is to be done, such as the erection of a church building, each group in it acts as a separate unit. Theoretically the bishop deals with the parish as a unit, but practically the congregations in it are distinct and recognizable units each of which must be treated separately.

Is there to be found in the New Testament, or in early church history, a church which had not its own proper ministers and its own proper rites and sacraments within itself? In these groups which we call churches only too often for three hundred and fifty or more days in the year there is no minister, no service, no sacrament. When the priest is urgently needed he is not there; and either he must be sought with difficulty, or the people must act without him. The members of such a church do not live in a church which is always present. Can we call this a church? Is it not rather a parody of a church?

The attitude of our bishops and clergy towards these groups is certainly in practice the attitude expressed to me by men in Canada, who told me that it was quite unnecessary that every little local group should have its own local ministers and its own local church life. If little groups have occasional services, that is all that they need and all that they can expect.

If it were true that this is all that they need, it is a great deal more than many groups can expect, for many lie outside the reach even of the itinerant clerics. It is notorious that there are many small groups of church people scattered all over the world which, as a matter of fact, do not and cannot have even occasional services because there are not enough itinerant clergy to give them even occasional services. There are large areas into which itinerant clergy have never been with any regularity. There are groups which have had no services for five, ten, or even twenty years. Even if we accept the principle that it is right for a large number of these so-called churches to be under the care of a single priest, we must recognize that the system breaks down most seriously in practice, because there are not sufficient clergy to supply even that. We are told, for instance, that 'consecutive work is difficult even in Khartoum with a British population of about five hundred: elsewhere it is impossible. Even big stations go unvisited for weeks and months. Out-stations can seldom be reached and the more distant ones never.'[1]

Where a cleric is in charge of a large number of these churches, we are constantly told that the people have a service once a month, or something of that sort, and we are constantly deceived. 'Once a month' may mean anything; what it scarcely ever means is perfect regularity for any length of time. The clergy are human beings liable to the infirmities of the flesh, and when they travel about from place to place to hold services, it is quite certain that from time to time they get delayed and the services are not held. When I was in Canada I made it my business to examine carefully into the meaning of this 'once a month' and found, in those cases where I could get exact information, that 'once a month' was anything but a precise statement of the facts. In one case where the bishop told me that a priest went once a month for a certain period, I found that, as a matter of fact, the man had never set foot in the building for the whole of the period. I found that perfect regularity was, as one might expect, impossible. When I say this I am not casting any slur at all upon the devotion and energy of devoted and energetic men: I am simply saying that they are not absolute masters of conditions. They cannot avoid sickness, and they cannot avoid mishaps, and when we are told that people receive services once a month we must take that into account.

A little while ago a bishop in South Africa wrote that he had at last succeeded in securing that all the congregations in his diocese should be visited by a priest to administer the Holy Communion once a quarter. When I went into that diocese the first man to whom I spoke said: 'I will tell you the name of a place where that is cer-

[1] *World Call*, vol. V, p .112,

tainly not true.' Arrangements of that kind can never be true for any length of time.

Infrequent services, irregular services, teach men to do without any. They grow accustomed to Sundays without services. For three Sundays out of four there is no service. The lesson taught on those three cannot be undone in one. The people forget on which Sunday the cleric is due, and they arrange a picnic or a tennis party. They learn to do without any religious services, and then when they have learnt that lesson the cleric is distressed and troubled, because they do not heed his exhortations and entreaties to attend.

The people learn also another lesson. They learn to think that church life consists in church going. We offer them 'services' instead of the fellowship of the church. The church cannot be a society in which they live all their lives. It has no local existence for them as a village is a local entity for those who live in it. The church seems to appear and disappear with the arrival and departure of the cleric, and church life seems to consist in attending the services, and is, like the services, intermittent. But that is surely not what church life was meant to be. The church was once a society in which men lived, not merely an organization for providing services which they might, or might not, attend. Men lived in the society of the church and enjoyed in the church all the warmth of a society and not merely the advantage of occasional services.

The value of that local union in a local church we have lost because our stipendiary system makes the proper constitution of the church in small groups impossible. Consequently it is not surprising if our people look upon attendance at church as a purely private matter and the baptism of their children as a purely private matter, and then it is not a long step to thinking that, if they turn on the wireless receiver and listen to some hymns and a sermon, it is as good as, if not better than, joining with their fellows in the worship of God in their own church.

Under this system there must be a constant supply of young and vigorous men to take up the work. The itinerant cleric can establish nothing which can abide if he is removed and a successor is not at hand. Everything depends upon him. There can be no sacraments, no church life without him, and he cannot ensure that his successor will be at hand when he retires. If he goes, those people will be left destitute, as destitute as if he had never been. Most men do not seem to realize that at all; but I have seen it happen. I have stood upon the ruins of years of hard work. Some men do realize it, and to them it is a nightmare. It is a grief quite unknown to clergy in large towns where it is certain that another cleric can always be found. In town churches men often fear that their successor may unbuild much that they have tried to build up; but they do not fear that all regular organized church life will come to an end. But in the most needy, the most out-of-the-way places, that is exactly what may happen, and sometimes does happen, because the supply of clergy to take up these tasks of itincrating in thc country is not constant.

16

Teaching

When I have urged the necessity of establishing the local church with its own ministers and its own local observance of Christ's sacraments, I have often met with the response: 'You lay too much stress on the sacraments and you ignore the ministry of teaching; you say that communicants untrained in theological colleges could be ordained priests, and celebrate the Holy Communion, and lead the local church; but you ignore the necessity of teaching. Untrained priests could not teach.' I have heard men talk about the creation of a class of 'masspriests.' I have heard more than one bishop speak as though the ordination of voluntary clergy would be the creation of a body of men ordained to celebrate holy mysteries, but not to teach. The question, then, of the teaching of the church in dioceses overseas is one of great importance to our present discussion.

Let us begin by considering the present position in the scattered groups overseas. Let us first look at those groups which no priest ever visits regularly. What teaching do they now receive? None at all. Now suppose that a bishop visited such a group, and, finding there one or two faithful men, ordained them to minister to themselves and their neighbours. The argument before us maintains that those men are not sufficiently trained to preach the Faith or to teach one another; but that they are sufficiently godly and sufficiently well educated to celebrate. The bishop who uses it is taking it for granted that he would license men to celebrate, but not to preach or to teach. These men, then, would celebrate: the little congregation would enjoy the sacraments of Christ; they would live in an organized church where services were duly held; but no one would be licensed to preach.

I ask, then, would they not be better off, even in the matter of teaching, under those circumstances than they are now, when they have nothing at all? Putting the preaching of sermons on one side, it is impossible to imagine that these priests would not read the services of Matins and Evensong as well as celebrate: for no bishop would license a man to celebrate and not to read Matins and Evensong. Is there, then, no teaching in our services of Morning and Evening

Prayer apart from the sermon? Is there no teaching in our Office of Holy Communion apart from the sermon? I cannot conceive any man maintain that argument. Whatever one may say of a Mass celebrated in a language which the people do not understand, or of Offices repeated in a language which the people do not understand, I think that it is quite impossible to maintain that the reading of our services of Morning and Evening Prayer, with their regular Biblical lessons, are not full of teaching of the very highest order, or that the celebration of the Holy Communion according to our Liturgy is not teaching of the very highest order.

Again, would these priests of whom the bishop is thinking not prepare their children and the children of members of their congregation for Confirmation, and, in preparing them, would they not teach them the Church Catechism? I can scarcely imagine a bishop ordaining a priest and refusing to allow him to prepare children for Confirmation by teaching them the Catechism. But is not that teaching, and teaching of a very high order? I know that someone may be found to say that such men could teach the Church Catechism, but could not teach it intelligently because they have not been to a theological college; but the objection seems to me simply absurd. Children are extremely well prepared for Confirmation by people who have not been to a theological college. The Church Catechism is not unintelligible to people of ordinary intelligence.

Putting the case, then, at its very worst, it seems to me that the gain is wholly on one side; but, as a matter of fact, that extreme statement of the case is exaggerated. If we look at the expansion of some of those strange sects which are spreading overseas, we see that their local leaders are not men trained in special colleges, yet we cannot possibly say that men who join those sects receive no instruction. The members of them are often well instructed in their religion, and they nearly all get their instruction for themselves. We may say that the teaching is erroneous, but that is not to the point. The point is that, where people join these sects, they do not remain ignorant of the teaching of the sect. They do not remain ignorant, largely because it is impossible for them to rely on a teacher who turns up once a month or once a quarter, but are compelled to hold their own services and instruct themselves and one another from literature provided at their own expense. Why should we imagine that church people alone, when put into a position to hold their own proper services, would

learn nothing and teach one another nothing, or, if they learnt anything, would learn only heresy? Is there any reason whatsoever for
that assumption? As a matter of fact, a large number would be men
of good education, and the most ignorant could read, and there are
excellent manuals which the bishops could recommend. Why should
churchmen alone be so utterly obtuse that they can learn nothing for
themselves, and must depend entirely upon the sermons of a man who
has had a year or two's training in a theological college? Would
ordination incline them to wish to know nothing? On the contrary,
the position of authority and responsibility would certainly move
them to inquire and to learn more than they have ever known before.
No one can doubt it.

I suggest that the Bible itself is a book of teaching for the church,
and might be read as such, not in snippets, but in large complete
passages. One priest in Canada told me that he read to his people the
lives of the patriarchs and the prophets and the life of our Lord as
complete biographies, and that years afterwards he had been told
that more profit had been derived from those readings than from
any sermons that he had preached. I suggest that bishops might send
books of instruction in the Faith, sound theological writings, to voluntary clergy, who, like my friends, did not feel able to preach, and
that from such connected reading the whole congregation would
derive immense benefit.

The question of teaching is really not the difficulty. The difficulty
is that church people are taught to rely entirely upon somebody else
to provide everything for them. The ordination of voluntary clergy
would break down that deplorable habit in the local churches. And
many more men than we imagine, not only could, but would, read
and prepare and preach very good sermons if they felt themselves
responsible for the religious life of their local church. The sermons
might not indeed be the type of theological sermon with which we
are familiar, but they would be extremely practical and closely re-
lated to the life of the little community from which they sprang. They
would be far more intelligible to their hearers than many of the sermons preached by the clergy trained in the theological schools.

When it is a question of ordaining voluntary clergy untrained in
theological colleges, this question of preaching is always thrust into
the foreground as an objection; but when it is a question of appointing lay readers, the very men who say that they could not trust a

voluntary cleric to teach because he has not been to a theological college, appoint a lay reader to do that very thing, in spite of the fact that he has not been to a theological college. They attempt to establish the church on the basis of lay preachers, while they argue that they cannot establish the church with the proper ministers because there are no men capable of preaching.

IV

PERSONAL STYLE

The extracts contained in this chapter come from matter in Roland Allen's papers that was not published in his lifetime. They include the open letter explaining his resignation from the parish of Chalfont St Peter in 1907 which was included in *The Ministry of the Spirit* (1960), as well as correspondence and a portion of an unfinished manuscript ("The Family Rite") that were first published in *Reform of the Ministry* (1968). These personal writings illustrate in various ways the context in which Allen did his thinking, the ways in which he sought to spread his ideas, and some of the conclusions to which he was finally led.

17

To the Parishioners of Chalfont St Peter

CHALFONT ST PETER.

My Friends, *November 25th, 1907*

I am very anxious that you should all understand the reason why I am resigning my work here.

From the earliest times the Church has always asserted her right to ordain the conditions on which she admits people to her privileges and to reject those who deliberately and persistently break her laws, which are the laws of God. This principle is definitely asserted in several places (see the rubrics before the Holy Communion and the Burial Offices) and tacitly implied everywhere in our own Prayer Book. But in process of time it has come to pass in England that on the one hand nearly everybody in the country is, at least in name, Christian, and on the other hand the machinery by which the law of the Church was intended to be made effective has fallen into disuse, and in practice it is now almost impossible to enforce it. Thus the widest inclusion of every kind and class of man has been accompanied with a relaxation of the means by which the morality of the society was maintained. The result is that it has become customary for people who make no profession of believing the doctrines of the Church, or who make no profession of keeping the laws of the Church, to demand and use her offices as if they were theirs by natural inheritance.

In consequence we see the strange and painful sight of men and women who habitually neglect their religious duties, or who openly deny the truth of the Creeds, or who by the immorality of their lives openly defy the laws of God, standing up as sponsors in a Christian church, before a Christian minister, in the presence of a Christian congregation and as representatives of the Church on behalf of a new-born child solemnly professing their desire for Holy Baptism, their determination to renounce the world, the flesh and the devil, their stedfast faith in the Creed and their willingness to obey God's holy will, whilst they know, and everyone in the church knows, that they themselves neither do, nor intend to do, any of these things. Then they are solemnly directed to see that the child is taught the faith and practice which they set at nought. Or again, we see that sad sight of the dead body of a man who all his life denied the claim of Jesus

Christ, or who set at nought the moral laws of God, brought into Christ's church in order that a service may be read over his body which, whilst alive, he utterly scorned.

I am, of course, aware that no priest is legally bound to admit any but communicants as sponsors, but immorality of life is no bar to the legal use of the Burial or Marriage Services. In the one case the law, in the other custom (more powerful often than law) compels the acquiescence of a priest in a practice which he cannot justify.

For no one can justify these things. They undermine the fundamental principle that the Church stands for morality of life; they suggest the horrible doctrine that the Church does not regard morality as an essential part of religion. They embolden men to go on living in sin in the hope that they will not be rejected at the last. Ignorant men speak as if Christ and His Church had nothing to offer which is not the natural inheritance of every Englishman, nor any right to lay down rules and conditions on which those gifts may be obtained; because they see every man, whatever his belief or his character, admitted without question to the highest privileges which the Church can bestow.

They bring the services of the Church into disrepute and make them an open scorn. There is a horrible danger in using holy services in the case of people who deny by word or deed all that is implied in them. People think and speak as if the services of the Church were 'mere forms.' God is not mocked. Services used in the name of God are high and holy things, sources of real blessing, and to degrade them into 'mere forms' is a serious offence, of which the consequences are terribly real.

Now, as parish priest, it is my duty to uphold morality and to defend religion, and I feel that in acquiescing in these customs I am neither upholding morality nor defending religion. I cannot satisfy my conscience by exhorting people to refrain from doing what is wrong, and then in the last resort, if they will not listen to me, giving way to them. I have done that, I fear, too often. I have carried my exhortations to the point of seriously annoying some of you. I have entreated and advised till we both were weary, but you knew and I knew that in the end I could not absolutely refuse. In one or two cases I regret that I did not refuse; but my mind was not clear as to the right course, and I preferred to obey the law. Now I am clear: I cannot and will not do these things any longer.

I am well aware of the serious character of my decision. I am not ignorant that I cannot act as I am determined to act, and yet hold any benefice in England. It has indeed been urged upon me by some that I might retain my position and wait until some serious case arose and I was forced by law to resign. I feel sure that I could, if I would, do that. I believe that so long as I acted wisely and discreetly, I should enjoy again, as I have enjoyed in the past, the sympathy and support of every communicant in this church. But that would not be right. Legal processes are not easily understood by the poor and ignorant, and some of those who would most bitterly resent my refusal to obey the law are very poor. I will not do in the case of a poor man an action for which he cannot force me to pay the legal penalty. I think the poor man would feel a just resentment if he were treated in spiritual matters in a way which a rich man could resist by process of law. And more than that, it seems to me scarcely honest to hold and enjoy the emoluments of an office of which I deliberately refuse to perform the legal obligations.

If that were not enough I should be compelled to resign by my sense of the very serious nature of resistance to law. I believe that passive resistance to law is sometimes a duty, but I do not believe that it is a light matter or one to be undertaken without the most serious consideration and the most deliberate determination to bear cheerfully the penalty whatever the penalty may be. A passive resistance which costs little or nothing is a passive resistance which I despise and dread. It tends to undermine an authority which the Bible tells us proceeds from God, and it is only justified by the strongest moral obligations and the most complete self-surrender to serious consequences. For me to resist the law whilst I enjoyed my office, trusting to your sympathy and support to save me from the consequences, would be, in my opinion, to commit that offence.

One form of protest, and only one, remains open to me, and that is to decline to hold an office in which I am liable to be called upon to do what I feel to be wrong. I have chosen that. I have resigned.

There remains one serious objection to all that I have said and it is an objection of which I am profoundly sensible. You are all well aware that a great many good and thoughtful men hold these positions and perform these offices without reproach, and you know that one will be found to take my place when I am gone. I am very anxious to explain this so far as I can. For the past three years I have been restrained from taking any action solely by the feeling that I must be wrong in refusing to do what so many good men can conscientiously do. I felt that I could not face the charge that I was setting myself up to be better and wiser than these men when in very truth I knew that I was not. They argue, if I understand them rightly, that they can do more good by continuing in their cures to perform these offices than by any other course. They hope to raise the standard of public opinion in these matters by continual teaching, and they can point to many signs that the standard of opinion is being so raised. They believe that it is their duty in a world of imperfection, to tolerate the imperfection which they cannot remove whilst they strive after the perfection which they desire. They think that refusal to perform these services is contrary to law, and that to resign rather than to obey is a counsel of despair which would reduce all church work in England to chaos. They plead that acts done by the ministers of the Church are done in the name and with the authority of the whole Church, and that therefore no individual priest can be held individually responsible for acts so done. They say that the Church as a matter of history has never been free from these difficulties; that we must look forward to the quiet growth of an enlightened public opinion, and that meanwhile it is the duty of a good minister to do his best under the conditions in which he now finds himself.

These arguments are sufficient to satisfy the minds of many good men: I can only say that they do not satisfy me. I have repeatedly told you from this pulpit that I believe we ought always at all costs to act according to the dictates of our conscience—that when our conscience tells us that a thing is wrong we ought not to do it whatever the consequences may be. When a difficult question arises, when our conscience protests against some action which is commonly done by a great many good men, I think we ought carefully to inquire whether our conscience is well informed (for a conscience may be morbid or misinformed), we ought to take time and pains to make sure that we are not suffering from a delusion; but if after all that careful examination our conscience still persists in forbidding us to do it, we must obey. It is better to do anything, to suffer anything, rather than to live under the condemnation of that voice which speaks to us with the authority of God.

And I believe further that in the end it will be found that no man can better fulfil his duty to others than by strictly observing that rule. It may appear now as if obedience to conscience and the service of the church in this place were in opposition, that to obey conscience in resigning is to abandon all hope of useful work. But I am persuaded that in the end it will be made plain that these two things which now appear to be in opposition are really one, and that I can do no service to you so true as to refuse to serve you in this. I believe that Christ's teaching about simplicity of aim, singleness of eye, is directed to just such difficulties as these; that He meant to teach us to refuse to be blinded by doctrines of expediency, by side issues; to do simply and obediently what He tells us, and that if we do that we shall find that in the end we have not missed the other. I believe that in resigning I am seeking not merely my own salvation, but your best interests and the interests of the church of which I am a minister.

I resign with very deep regret. I have valued most highly your sympathy, your forbearance, your ungrudging help, and as time goes on, I shall more and more feel the loss of it.

I have asked the Bishop to declare the vacancy at Christmas, and I have asked the patrons, S. John's College in Oxford, to use all possible urgency that is agreeable with care in seeking the right man to supply my place.

Till Christmas I shall continue my work here. Then I must seek work where it may please God to call me.

Meanwhile, I commend myself, the Bishop, the patrons and the parish to your earnest prayers. You will pray, I am sure, for me, that I may be guided aright. You will pray that it may please God to send to this parish a faithful and true pastor.

And this may He do for His mercy's sake.

Believe me,

Your sincere friend,

ROLAND ALLEN

This letter explains itself. It is included not only for its biographical interest, but also because the issues which Allen raised are now, more than fifty years later, very much alive, not least under the form of 'baptismal rigorism.'

18

Correspondence with the Bishop of Central Tanganyika

From The Times, *April* 10, 1930
The Church in Tanganyika

To: The Editor of *The Times*
Sir,

The British Mandated Territory of Tanganyika presents unique opportunities for Empire development in fulfilment of the condition laid down in the Mandate that the Mandatory 'shall undertake to promote to the utmost the material and moral well-being and the social progress of its inhabitants'.

The new Diocese of Central Tanganyika created in 1927 is seeking to co-operate with the Government in the realization of this fundamental clause. The Church in Australia has responded to the call of Empire, and thirty Australians supported by Australian money, have joined the English men and women working there. The late Archbishop Lord Davidson said: 'It has been a real encouragement to our sense of fellowship throughout the Anglican Communion that . . . Australia is sharing our grave responsibilities for the Christianization of East Africa and for the Church life there in years to come.'

In education 'equipment for life in the country' is our aim. The Government has incorporated the report of one of our schools in one of its own reports to the League of Nations as showing how fully the need of the African is being met and how suited to his condition is the type of education which he is receiving. Christian schools of this kind are the great hope of Africa. Tanganyika needs many more.

The uplift of the African involves not only education but medical work on a large scale. Child mortality in Tanganyika is eighty per cent. Two doctors and ten nurses on the diocesan staff last year treated 100,000 sick, saving the lives of very many mothers and children. The tragedy today is that medical supplies for their work are exhausted and there are no available funds for more. At two leper settlements the Church is doing her part to stamp out leprosy from this corner of the British Empire.

Further, though the diocese is nearly five times the size of England and Wales, there is not an Anglican Church of Europeans anywhere. I am anxious to build ten churches as strategic centres for the officials who are guiding and controlling the native authorities and the destiny of the whole people and also for planters, miners and commercial men who are developing the resources of the country.

Sir Horace Byatt, KCMG, the former Governor of Tanganyika, stated: 'The Empire follows its sons with protection of life and property. It is just as imperative to follow them with protection of the soul.' Twenty thousand pounds are needed at once to enable us to continue to co-operate with the Government in this educational and medical work, as well as to build the ten churches for Europeans, which will include a stone cathedral at Dodoma. British honour demands that we shall do our 'utmost'.

Yours hopefully,

G.A. Central Tanganyika[1]

Gifts marked 'Central Tanganyika Diocesan Fund' may be sent to the Bishop of Central Tanganyika, 76 Onslow Gardens, S.W.7. or to Barclay's Bank, 108 Queen's Gate, S.W.7.

To the Bishop of Central Tanganyika

April 10, 1930

My Lord Bishop,

In *The Times* today I read an appeal from you which moves me to write to you. In its matter and form it is very familiar to me because I have watched these appeals for over thirty years, and I know the misery of them. I do beg you to consider what they involve. Can you really build on that foundation? Many, many before you have tried to do so. Is there one of the overseas bishops who will gather at Lambeth who could not use and would not rejoice to get all that you ask? Can we possibly give them all that they need on that basis? Suppose that you succeed in getting what you ask, will

---

[1] [The Rt Revd G. A. Chambers was the first Bishop of Central Tanganyika, a new diocese created by the division of the diocese of Mombasa in 1927.]

not the use of it create a need for more? If you find the money where will you find the men? I do beg you to think that the way which you are going leads, as it has led others, to a perpetually increasing appeal which cannot be satisfied in full and ends in disappointment, some times almost in despair, or, what is almost as bad, in an uneasy conviction that they must just make the best of what they can get and leave the greater part of their dioceses either untouched or just touched from time to time. They do not like it, but they just admit that they cannot help it, and they are sick of making appeals which cannot satisfy. That is enough to break any bishop's heart. The Church becomes a sort of organization for supplying one or two hospitals, a few schools, a few church buildings, more or less regularly served and generally ill attended by Europeans, a few mission stations with their native converts round them all depending, in a very real sense depending, upon an outside source of supply for their existence, and from time to time retrenchment and withdrawal are inevitable.

Is there a single diocese overseas which is not in that case? And is not that inevitable when we build on the fluctuating response to appeals made outside the diocese? And meanwhile the whole country waits, the few earnest Christian souls are starved, and the heathen are unreached, and they *all* need the Church and need the Church badly, today. We cannot advance, we cannot satisfy the need, we cannot use the opportunity, because we are held up by the attitude of mind which makes any advance depend upon the success of an appeal for money, or for men, or for both, outside the diocese.

In a diocese like yours, surely you are in the position rather of an apostle than of a territorial bishop. You cannot do everything. You cannot educate the whole youth of your diocese, non-Christian and Christian alike. You cannot provide a medical service for the whole population, non-Christian and Christian alike. You cannot even supply church buildings for every group of Christians, nominal and practising, alike. Are you not in the position of an apostle? Then can you do your real work in other fashion than he did it?

In the life of St Paul we see how it was done: in the lives of many succeeding apostles. They knew that their *one* work was to establish the Church, and to establish the Church they needed *nothing* that was not before them on the spot. They needed Christian men: they were there in the persons of non-Christian men. They gathered together the souls whom God called, and they established them, ordaining elders among them to lead and to feed. The buildings followed inevitably — exactly as the converts of the Kroo Evangelist Harris created their own buildings in abundance. Everything followed, all that the Church needed she had, because all that she needed was there on the spot in the lives and possessions of those whom God called. There was no limit to advance, no need for an appeal for help to any outside source. There was life and growth on the spot. Surely that is how all great advance is made, not by importation, but by life present, expressing itself in growth. We must begin with souls not with buildings. Sure, surely, my Lord Bishop, the way of the Apostles is the right way. It is the way of life, growing and expanding without limit.

Believe me,

Yours sincerely,
Roland Allen

From the Bishop of Central Tanganyika

76 Onslow Gardens,
London, S.W.7.

My dear Mr Allen,   April 11, 1930

This is to acknowledge with thanks your letter and to express my appreciation of your point of view.

It is an ideal which I am seeking to follow, but supplementing it with outside help for the supply of medicines and for the building of churches in European centres.

Your letter is indeed a spur to foster and encourage 'life and growth on the spot'.

Yours sincerely,
G.A. Central Tanganyika

To the Bishop of Central Tanganyika

Amenbury,
Beaconsfield, Bucks
April 12, 1920

My Lord Bishop,

Please. Are you not deceiving yourself? You say, 'It is an ideal which I am seeking to follow but supplementing it with outside help for the supply of medicines, and for the building of churches in European centres'.

(1) Had that 'ideal' any place or expression in your letter to *The Times*? Obviously none. But why? Is it not because that ideal and your appeal are not in harmony? The appeal is not in line with the ideal. You cannot make the appeal in terms of the ideal. In making the appeal you, therefore, so far as it is concerned, ignore the ideal.

(2) But can a man really be seeking to follow an ideal when he pursues a course which compels him to ignore it? Can he follow by not following an ideal? Or is he really opposing the ideal to the practical, saying in his heart, 'No doubt that is the ideal course, but as a matter of practical politics I must set it aside as a rule of conduct in this case'. That surely is nothing else than our old enemy *Video meliora proboque, deteriora sequor*,[1] against which the pulpit thunders. I suppose that you, when in the pulpit, thunder against it and proclaim that the Gospel is a deliverance from it.

(3) But you say that you do follow the ideal, only that the appeal is a supplementary. Is that true? Then why did the appeal exclude the ideal? Is it not because the two are not in harmony? Can we possibly supplement the following of an ideal by the practice of something which excludes it? Could St Paul have supplemented his following of the ideal by an appeal for money and men to Antioch, or would such an appeal have proved that his ideal was a different ideal, and would not his appeal have altered the whole character of his work? How can you take out money to build churches for Europeans and by that act prove to them that you are following the ideal? That seems to me impossible, contradictory. Are you not really using the word 'supplementary' to deceive yourself? I can understand a man saying, 'That course might be, or even would be, ideal under other circumstances, but under the circumstances before me it is not ideal but impracticable nonsense', but I cannot understand his saying, 'It is an ideal of which I approve but I must supplement it by something which is only at home in a totally different ideal. I shall take action which will by its very nature compel me along a road divergent from the goal of which I have just expressed approval and at which I profess to aim'.

I know, I know well, how fatally easy it is to persuade ourselves that something which is not in harmony with our professed aim is

---

[1] [I see the better and approve it, but I follow the worse.]

yet only a supplementary necessity. The writings of moralists are full of warnings and examples. The way of the Apostles and the way of our overseas bishops are not the same: they do not lead to the same end, express the same ideal, and we cannot half go over from the one to the other. We must choose one or the other. The whole history of all our dioceses overseas has proved that we cannot supply churches for every group of Christians overseas, nor men to minister to them. Why should we choose this group or that? Why Tanganyika rather than Canada? There is no answer to that, there never has been, there cannot be, because the question ought never to have been raised at all. *All* groups which desire the Church and Church life ought to have Church life in its fullness. We can give it to all, but only on the apostolic basis. You can go to your people and say, 'I am here to find, or to lead into the light, men whom God has called. When I find them I will establish them. I am here to ordain, and in the Name of Christ, I will ordain. I shall not need buildings, you can easily settle that matter for yourselves, but I shall need churches and I shall establish those who will act as churches'. On that basis we need never talk of any choice such as that miserable choice which is now set before us, a dead choice. But we must choose which road we will take.

Your people will not understand you, if you speak with two voices. You ask for ten churches, suppose that you get money only for five. How will you choose? That choice ought never to be before you, and it cannot be before you, if you are out to establish churches rather than a Church, to ordain rather than lay foundation stones. When you say that you are out to establish churches your people will understand you. Some of them may not be prepared for such a bold and to them a novel idea, but they will understand it. Men have no difficulty in understanding it. But it is impossible to half say it and to be understood. The first necessity is to say it to ourselves so that we understand it and that is without reservations.

> *Believe me,*
> *Yours sincerely,*
> Roland Allen

19

The Family Rite

I was brought up in the Church of England, and for years and years I took things to be intellectually apprehended, and thought that the evidence was good and strong. Only the other day Priscilla objected that I did not read the Bible like other books. I protested that no one read any book which had exercised a profound influence on thought and belief like other books.[1] The weight of that reference [the manuscript adds "history" as an alternate here] rested on it. In the case of the Bible the weight was irresistible. Yet her word did not leave me. Almost insensibly I began to read St Paul with a difference. I felt it. Sayings which hitherto I had let go as subjects of merely archaistic interest assumed a new significance. My attitude towards the writer was changing. I was criticizing not merely the speech but its author.

There is all the difference in the world between that criticism and what is commonly called 'biblical criticism'. How deep is the gulf between reading the words of an 'inspired' writer, that is, looking in his words for the revelation of truth and regarding all that does not reveal that truth at once as unessential, to be passed by, or to await some later understanding, or deeper meaning to be grasped, and reading with the feeling that when his argument seems weak, the meaning of the word 'inspired' is changed for the man who sees, or thinks that he sees, the weakness! It is very easy to understand the attitude of the fundamentalist who says, 'If you question the absolute truth of any single word in the Bible, you are lost'.

Something of that sort happened to me in my study of the 'stipendiary system' in the Church. I began by questioning its wisdom, especially as it was applied in 'chaplaincies' and 'missions' overseas. Then I began to see that it was immoral: its practice overthrew the expressed teachings of its observers. The sayings in the Gospels about Scribes and Pharisees applied exactly. They set an ecclesi-

---

[1] I think that my answer to Priscilla was shallow. The point is that we do not apply our mind to the Bible as we apply it to other books. There is a somewhat that withholds, a restraint, something deeper than any recognition of respect due to the greatest and best books.

astical tradition above the law of God, which they yet professed to observe. They were self-condemned.

Anyone can understand what a shock the recognition of that fact must be to a man who has accepted the Church without question. Once seen, the fact shrieks aloud. It seems almost impossible that good men do not see it and hear it, yet they go on apparently unaffected by it. When I first saw it, I felt as if I must have gone mad. How could it possibly be that so many men, much wiser and more able than myself, could fail to have seen what was so plain to me? Were my eyes distorted? Was I the victim of some wild delusion?

But when I wrote *Missionary Methods: St Paul's or Ours?* no one argued that I was seeing the thing that was not. They did not say, 'The man is mad'; yet they did nothing. In spite of the fundamental character of the truth which I had set before them, they did nothing. The same issue followed all my later writings. I was compelled to the conclusion that I was not mad, and that the truth which I affirmed was a real truth which other men could see. But how did they see it? Now, after so long a time, I think that they saw it as a mere proposition expressing a moral judgment, but not as a compelling truth.

Of course I can remember how, when I was ordained, such an idea had never entered my head. I took the Church and its ordering as fixed settled facts of life; though even then I was horrified when I heard some clergy talking of 'preferment' as something which they coveted, in connection with a 'good living' which was vacant. Still, the order was something which I did not question at all. Now, I suppose that men to whom I presented the moral objection to the stipendiary system annulling the Church and the Gospel, were so established in the tradition that nothing really shook them. The crust was so thick that a truth admitted did not penetrate to the springs of action. It remained on the surface until it dropped off. Only so can I reconcile my conviction that they were good men with their apparent inability to see that a moral issue so fundamental had any bearing upon conduct or made any call for penitence.

I suppose that the good men amongst the Scribes and Pharisees in Christ's day were in that case. They heard His denunciation of the Tradition, but it did not penetrate. Familiarity and habit were too strong. So when men did not dispute the truth of what I wrote, or said, of the ecclesiastical tradition which today annuls the doctrine which it was first established to protect, they know the truth, but only with their heads, not with their hearts; and so in them it dies.

I think it was the shock which I received at seeing the opposition between the teaching of the Church and the observance of a tradition which annulled the teaching that induced in me such a distrust of human intelligence as to amount almost to contempt.[1]

I knew, of course, that many of these men were far abler and better men than I was, yet I could not doubt the truth which I saw. They did not deny it. They did not dispute it; but it had no apparent effect on them. I wrote then under a sort of compulsion, expecting to achieve nothing by my labour. I no doubt found some pleasure in arranging my argument and facing every question that I could imagine, or hear, connected with it; but the despair induced by the conviction that nothing would come of it, was none the less horrible.

Slowly I began to think of the Church of England, perhaps even 'Christianity' as known to us, as something temporary, a stage in the history of religion, and local. It was plainly incapable of any universality. Even in England itself, as a system it was palpably breaking down. Roman Catholicism made great claims to solve the difficulty by infallible utterances, but I soon saw that it was simply a form of ecclesiastical Nazism, and could no more endure than political Nazism could endure. Sooner or later, unless all education is denied to them, men begin to think for themselves, but in a Nazi system every man must think, or at least speak, what he is told by leader or pope. Anything else breaks up the whole system. Claims made by a few English bishops and priests to hold the position of the Romans seemed to me simply ridiculous.

If Christianity as represented by the Church of England is only a stage in religious history, as Jewish Monotheism grew out of Henotheism and Henotheism grew out of Polytheism, what ought to be the attitude of a Christian towards it? A good Englishman supports the Government, however much he may criticize it. Ought a good

---

[1] The effect of this sort of distrust of human intelligence is to make one doubt whether any truth is known to us, or attainable. At best we seem to attain partial and more or less distorted truth. 'We see in a glass, darkly'. That may be a hope of better things to come, but it may be a root of despair. When human beings deny in act what they profess to know, it is very disturbing. When they cling more fast to a tradition or habit than to the truth which they profess, it works in the mind a sense of fundamental untruth. *Nothing* remains secure.

Christian Englishman to support the Church of England in that same way, as the form accepted by the majority? I suppose that a good many men do that, and I can understand a layman doing so. The Church of England may be full of contradictions and in practice deny its own doctrine, but it is still the best Christian institution known to us, and its destruction would be now no gain. Neither religion nor morality would profit by it. But for one ordained in the stipendiary order it is not so simple.

When I was serving at St Mark's, Nairobi, I told the congregation that for them to seek for one of the few stipendiaries for themselves was manifest spiritual selfishness. They were trying to keep for themselves what was needed quite as much, or much more, by others. They were looking solely on their own things, which the Apostle told them not to do. I told them that they could well supply their own services, and in so doing they would open a door for every congregation in the world to have its own proper services, which would indeed be looking on the things of others. I said that I would not continue to encourage them in their selfishness, nor pander to it, that it was not true Christian charity to help men to remain in a feeble selfish dependence when they could with a little effort escape from it, and that I must refuse to do that.

That action put me outside.[1] I could no longer assist the stipendiary system. But then could I, as a priest, accept the ministration of stipendiary clergy under the present circumstances. When I declined to assist, could I accept? I thought that hardly decent. So I took to celebrating at home with B., as I should have liked to see every father of a family doing where there was no public organized service. The trouble was that I did it where there was; but then, as I said, I was in a cleft stick. I knew that I was muddled.[2]

Side by side with this muddle went the biblical question I had long disputed, the 'authority' of the Church of England. Criticism and acceptance of authority are incompatible. When once a man begins to criticize, his reverence for the authority is broken; and

[1] It is noteworthy that Christ never seems to have expected that his denunciations would convert Scribes and Pharisees.

[2] A man who as a good Englishman supports the Government is not in quite the same position as the man who joins the Government and takes office. Men do not think it moral for a man who thinks that the Government is leading the nation astray to hold office in it. I was certain that the stipendiary system here was destroying the Church; how then could I openly attach myself to the Bishop's party?

criticism, which may begin with a detail, advances rapidly. I began to see that I had accepted the authority of the Bible as I had accepted the authority of the Church. My forbears had been members of the Church of England; they had treated the Bible as an inspired book, the Word of God. The 'Church Universal' had so accepted it. I had no reason to question it. If others questioned it, I answered that such universal acceptance was sufficient authority. So the Church was proved by the Bible, the Bible by the Church.

Now I do not think that argument so absurd as it looks. There is more behind it than simply setting the watch by the clock and the clock by the watch, more simply accepting the authority of the Bible on the witness of the Church, and the authority of the Church on the witness of the Bible.[1] Yet, once a man begins to criticize one, he begins to criticize the other, and his attitude is changed. Take, e.g., a passage like that in which Christ argues that there can be no offence in His claim to be the Son of God because in the Psalms men are called Gods. I suppose no one now ever reads that without some discomfort. I used to pass over it as 'a difficult passage'; but that was all. The point was that I passed over it.[2] But let a man once cease to pass over difficult passages, and then what happens? Serious consequences follow, just as serious consequences follow the ceasing to pass over the significance of the stipendiary traditions in the Church. Similarly, in reading St Paul's Epistles let a man once recognize that he is reading logical arguments and deal with them as logical arguments; will he not find here and here that the argument will not stand?

I found, then, one authority, the Church which practised, and by its practice taught, what was false by its own theory: I found another, the Bible, which was inconsistent. Some of it I could accept, some of it I could not. The simple plan of following critics who denied the genuineness of difficult passages seemed to me childish. The Bible was accepted by the Church as a whole, as it stands. It seemed to me quite reasonable to compare copies and versions and

[1] More, because the fallacy breaks down unless the witness in each case depends wholly and solely upon the other.

[2] The eschatological discourses in the Gospels did suggest that Jesus expected His return after His death in glory to be speedy and the explanations were inadequate. This and the manifest conviction of the early preachers confirmed it. Christ was to return in the clouds attended by the heavenly host, very soon; and He Himself had said so.

to prefer one statement or form of statement to another on strictly textual grounds; but to cut out whole chunks on any other grounds seemed to me a false method of dealing with the book. On the other hand, to accept as equally divinely inspired the book Ecclesiastes and the Sermon on the Mount was absurd. Some parts of the Bible, then, I treated as historical romance, or ancient stories thrown into literary form, with deep underlying religious import; others like passages in St Paul's Epistles expressed directly spiritual and moral truths which hit me like pistol shots.

What then? Was my religion a purely individual thing? Was I to be to myself sole judge of what I would accept? Was I, who knew that other men, much wiser and more learned than myself, had gone far astray, to set myself up as sole authority for myself? Alter, even a little, some element in my birth and upbringing, and I might be taking a very different view. To decide great religious issues for myself was plainly a very dangerous and slippery business. But I was compelled to do it. I could not escape. Wherever I could, and that was generally on points which did not hit me hard, I accepted the authority of the Church, or of learned men who seemed to speak for the Church; but where I was really touched, I was convinced by my own inside. I was simply compelled to do that. I had no choice.

Take for instance, the use of sacraments. So far as I know, I am the only priest of the Church of England who has practised the celebration of Holy Communion as a family institution deliberately and advisedly. My experience then has taught me much of which I was before ignorant. I had always been convinced that, in the beginning, Christians observed the Rite in their houses, as the Passover had been observed as a family rite, but that very soon, on the basis of the conviction that all Christians were brethren, and that there was *one* family in Christ, those who could, in any one place, met together, as one family, to observe it. So it became the Rite of a group, a local Church, and for that Church elders, or priests, were ordained and appointed, who in the service took the place of the Father in the family. Then, as the numbers and wealth of the Christian community increased, inevitably the Rite took on the form of a Temple Rite, its ornaments elaborated, its form stereotyped down to the minutest detail, till we reach the artificial rubrics of some of the Greek Rites.

By this way the elders or bishops of the early days became a body of professional clergy over against the laymen. They alone knew the Temple secrets. They were the doctors, lawyers, scribes of the Church. In their conclaves they spoke in the name of the Church. They were, and sometimes called themselves, 'The Church'. (Obviously their stronghold was in the sacraments which were 'necessary for salvation', and for long only the clergy could perform them. Not only the Holy Communion but Baptism also was performed only by the bishop or the priest; for to admit a soul into the Church was as important a matter as to give him Communion in it. Both alike became Temple Rites; but in our day Baptism has largely ceased to be a priestly function. Deacons perform it, and laymen, though they seldom do, yet can perform it without offence.)

Now a Temple Rite, performed by professional ministers, is a very different thing from a Family Rite. It is more than a development; it is a transformation. Men who think it a development only, argue that the Church is the Spirit-bearing body and was divinely guided in this as in all other developments. I, who saw that it was a transformation which had led to the exclusion of the laity from any part in the sacrament except where the priest was to be found, regarded it as an illegitimate change resulting from an accession of wealth and a natural grasping after power on the part of the clerical order in the Church.[1]

When I began to celebrate the Holy Communion at home with my wife as a regular thing, I began by thinking of the act as a performance of the Temple Rite as it might be in the private chapel of a great house; but by degrees I felt instinctively that the vestments and ritual of a private chapel were out of place, perhaps because I had no chapel. So gradually I began to drop them, until I reached the point where I abandoned them altogether. Then I slowly realized more and more clearly that I had in fact returned to the Family Rite, and I liked it and approved of it. I still used the form prescribed in the Prayer Book, because I was sure that I could not better it; but I did not follow it slavishly.

[1] It seemed to me to be a reversion to a lower and more humanly convenient form. Just as the Israelites were constantly in danger of reverting to idolatry and the worship of familiar deities, deities familiar to their ancestors, so this 'development' was really a reversion from the higher to the lower, from the priesthood of the Christian which made great demands to the priesthood of an Order which lightened those demands.

If we agreed (and we consulted together) that some other Epistle or Gospel than that prescribed in the book was desirable at that time, we changed it. When we were, as generally happened, by ourselves, we omitted the recital of the Ten Commandments. I did not adhere to Rubrics which bade me stand up or kneel at certain times; being old, I often sat. I stood, or knelt, as my sense of reverence bade me, being convinced that God sees the heart. In fact, I realized that I was performing a Family Rite and acted accordingly. I was in truth doing what I had long urged Christian people to do when they were separated from any organized Church. The fact that I was ordained took little place in my thought, for I was doing what I wished all Christian heads of households to do.

The only difference lay in the fact that I was near enough to a church where the sacrament was observed. That I did not attend the service there was partly for the reason which I set out before, that in the Cathedral I was a member of the Order and, as such, should there minister, if I attended, and I was utterly opposed to the clericalism which denied the Rite to men up country who could not support a stipendiary, partly because I disliked the manner in which the sacrament was ministered there, and partly, for aught that I know (for such secrets are hidden from me) from some other, even less worthy motives; but I am sure in the main because I was feeling my way back to the Family Rite.[1]

I believe that if I were beginning all over again I should, at least I hope that I should, not have been ordained into a stipendiary order which holds the Rite as its own prerogative at all, but should have celebrated the Rite as head of my family at the breakfast or supper table and let the breakfast or supper follow it.

I am convinced that any knowledge in such matters must be gained by practical experience. Mere theorizing, or mere study of ancient practice, is not enough. And the practice must be long, and it would be better if the effect were observed in many cases. It must be long, because anything new is apt to produce an effect by its very newness. It is unfamiliar, and its unfamiliarity demands attention such as the familiar may lose by its very familiarity. The immediate effect produced by unfamiliarity may offend or attract

---

[1] I have never in my life been able to convince myself that I did any act from one pure motive. I might think at the time that I did, but it would not bear examination.

unduly, and the offence or attraction may be lost later, as the attraction is slackened or relaxed by familiarity.   *en*

As I said, I moved towards the Family Rite slowly and by degrees.
I might have stopped, or turned back, at any moment, but the
further I went in that direction the more I was attracted that way.
I went slowly and in ignorance whither I went, till reflection on
what I was doing showed me where I was. I arrived before I knew
that I had arrived.

The hallowing of the family life by the Rite seems to me *now* the
vital point. The Church as seen today is too vague and amorphous.
There is no close attachment. At any given celebration no one knows
who will be present, or why. Attendance becomes an individualistic
act. No doubt there remains some sense of a Body, but it is ill-
defined. When the Rite is a Family Rite, there is inevitably a reality
present and a definiteness, and that definiteness does not destroy
the sense of the wider Body; it assists it, and would assist it more
if the celebration by many families was a familiar fact which Christians found whenever they went to visit another Christian family.
We should then not lose the Communion of Saints everywhere: on
the contrary, we should know and feel it more keenly than we do
now. It is the particular which helps us to reach the universal. To
try to jump straight to the universal when the particular has no
clear existence is too hard for most of us.

When I said that I had arrived, of course all that I meant, or
ought to have meant, was that I had arrived at a recognizable point,
not that I had reached anything like a terminus. I am very conscious
that I am moving. For one thing, I have not reached a proper
Family Rite. I celebrate with my wife, and with John when he is
here,[1] but what about Valerie and my servants? Valerie, however
much she may want to become a Christian, is not yet baptized, my
servants do not understand English. Consequently I cannot attain
to a full Family Rite, and I cannot experience it properly. But I
have experienced it to the limit of my capacity and opportunity;
and so far it is good.

I said that I began by questioning the practice of the Church. I
did this first in China when I saw that our restriction of Orders
barred progress, and made the Church a foreign institution gov-

---

[1] Occasionally a visitor staying in the house has joined us. B. says that they have
been impressed.

erned by foreigners: then in the Colonies, by not only barring progress, but also revealing that our whole relation to the sacraments
was chaotic and contradictory and putting us exactly into the position of the Pharisees in the Gospels who let their tradition bring
to nought the commands which they were supposed to support.

Then I began to question my own position as an ordained priest.
The authority of the Church being shaken there follows a shaking
of the authority of its ministers. Much of this was universally recognized long before I began to think of it.

There was a time when the clergy spoke with unquestioned authority, as I am told that Roman Catholic priests still do in their
dealings with the Irish in Ireland and in Liverpool and other great
centres to which ignorant labourers flock, as well as in their dealings
with Natives in their Missions all over the world. The word of the
priest must be obeyed, or the direst consequences will follow.

Nowadays the medical profession takes much the same attitude.
They do not ask men to follow their advice: they order them to do
so, and threaten them with the most serious consequences if they
do not. Already I think there are signs that that authority is being
shaken, but it is still for many as absolute as was the authority of
the priest in former days. Exorcism is an example of the decay.
Once, the priest ordered the evil spirit to depart, and any case of
failure could be explained as the result of a lack of faith in the
patient or his friends, or of some ritual error in the form used. Then
men began to question the efficacy of the treatment and the reality
of the supposed condition of the patient, and now we seldom hear
of any formal exorcism. The doctor took the place of the exorcist.

Now the doctor's authority is shaken, and psychoanalysts are in
a sense undermining the authority of the medical man in many
cases. Disease is seen to be much more closely connected with mental and spiritual states than the medical profession admitted. Obviously that does not imply any return to the authority of the priest,
as a doctor of the soul, and so of the body; but it does surely suggest
a weakening of the authority of the medical profession as the sole
authority in matters of health. Whither that will lead I cannot even
guess.

For the moment, at least, the authority of the priest is shaken,
both on the mental [the manuscript adds "spiritual" as an alternate
here] and on the physical side. He can no longer expect to be ad-

mitted as one speaking with authority, but only as an adviser on certain conditions and with many reservations; or else as the minister of a Body which requires certain definite services to be performed for it.

Inevitably I felt that, and equally inevitably, because I am slow-witted, it grew upon me slowly and by almost imperceptible degrees. I questioned the authority of the Church: I questioned my own as a priest in the Church. If the truth were known (and I have said that I am quite incapable of knowing it) I should not be surprised to find that an inner feeling of this incongruity, though I was not then conscious of it, was really quite a powerful motive in leading me to refuse to serve St Mark's and consequently in any other church. I did not know it at the time, and thought that the argument which I put before them was the whole; but now I am not so sure. Even if I had known for certain that this other motive was moving me, I could not have presented the argument as I did to that congregation, but still I should have known that I myself was wobbling, though that had nothing to do with them or with the argument that they were practising a spiritual selfishness in seeking to procure for themselves the services of a priest who, on their own admission, was equally, or more, needed by others.

Bibliography

1. Books by Roland Allen

The Siege of the Peking Legations. London: Smith, Elder, 1901.

Missionary Methods; St Paul's or Ours? London: Robert Scott, 1912. Reprinted, London: World Dominion Press, 1930, 1949, 1956. Reset, with a memoir by Alexander McLeish, London: World Dominion Press; Grand Rapids, Mich.: Wm. B. Eerdmans Publishing Co., 1962.

Missionary Principles. London: Robert Scott, 1913; New York: Fleming H. Revell, 1913, under title *Essential Missionary Principles.* London: World Dominion Press; Grand Rapids, Mich.: Wm. B. Eerdmans Publishing Co., 1964.

Pentecost and the World: The Revelation of the Holy Spirit in 'The Acts of the Apostles.' London: Oxford University Press, 1917.

Educational Principles and Missionary Methods: The Application of Educational Principles to Missionary Evangelism. London: Robert Scott, 1919.

Missionary Survey as an Aid to Intelligent Co-operation in Foreign Missions. (Written in collaboration with Thomas Cochrane.) London: Longmans, Green, 1920.

Voluntary Clergy. London: S.P.C.K., 1923.

The Spontaneous Expansion of the Church and the Causes which Hinder It. London: World Dominion Press, 1927. Reprinted in 1949 and 1956. Reset, with a memoir by Alexander McLeish, London: World Dominion Press; Grand Rapids, Mich.: Wm. B. Eerdmans Publishing Co., 1962.

Voluntary Clergy Overseas: An Answer to the Fifth World Call. Privately printed at Beaconsfield, 1928.

The Case for Voluntary Clergy. London: Eyre & Spottiswoode, 1930.

S. J. W. Clark: A Vision of Foreign Missions. London: World Dominion Press, 1937.

2. Posthumous Publications

The Ministry of the Spirit: Selected Writings of Roland Allen, with a memoir by Alexander McLeish. Edited by David M. Paton. London: World Dominion Press, 1960; Grand Rapids, Mich.: Wm. B. Eerdmans Publishing Co., 1962. Rev. ed., 1965.

Reform of the Ministry: A Study in the Work of Roland Allen. Edited by David M. Paton. London: Lutterworth Press, 1968. (This book contains a 'biographical and theological essay' by the editor, a history of the Survey Application Trust by Sir Kenneth Grubb, a list of the publications of the World Dominion Press, and an account of Allen's last years in

East Africa by Prof. Noel D. King, together with previously unpublished writings of Allen and correspondence by him or to him.)

3. *Related Interest*

Beyerhaus, Peter, and Henry Lefever. *The Responsibile Church and the Foreign Mission*. London: World Dominion Press; Grand Rapids, Mich.: Wm. B. Eerdmans Publishing Co., 1964.

Denniston, Robin, ed. *Part Time Priests: A Discussion*. London: Skeffington, 1960.

Donovan, Vincent. *Christianity Rediscovered: An Epistle for the Masai*. New York: Orbis; London: SCM Press, 1982.

McGavran, Donald A. *The Bridges of God: A Study in the Strategy of Missions*. London: World Dominion Press; New York: Friendship, 1955.

————. *How Churches Grow: The New Frontier of Mission*. London: World Dominion Press; New York: Friendship, 1959.

Paton, David M., ed. *New Forms of Ministry*. London: Edinburgh House Press, 1965. (International Missionary Council Research Pamphlet No. 12)

p. 47 (1927) - Do we now have (in e.g. Nigeria) a "native episcopate"?